A Relationship With God

Discovering Life Beyond Religion

Ken Schott

Published by 21st Century Christian

©2012 21st Century Christian

2809 Granny White Pike, Nashville, TN 37204

All rights reserved.

ISBN:978-0-89098-538-0

Cover design by Jonathan Edelhuber

This book is dedicated to Kenny and Terri. May your personal relationship with God continue to grow and deepen as you face the various stages of your lives.

TABLE OF CONTENTS

PREFACE

"I love those who love me and those who seek me find me" (Proverbs 8:17).

"Here I am! I stand at the door and knock. If anyone hears my voice and opens the door, I will come in and eat with him and he with me" (Revelation 3:20).

The God of the Bible seeks a relationship with people—imperfect people, sinful people like you and me. If you have gone to church all your life and feel like your relationship with God is unsatisfactory, this book was written for you. If you are disillusioned with the church or concerned about the exodus of young people from today's church, this book will speak to your heart. If you yearn for a closer relationship with God, the chapters that follow were written to inspire you and help you find a more meaningful relationship. If you are angry, frustrated, or turned off by organized religion, God still wants to have a relationship with you. Hallelujah.

A walk through any book store reveals a plethora of religious authors who have written about God. Popular names such as Joyce Meyer, Max Lucado, Joel Ostean, Charles Stanley, Philip Yancey, Rick Warren, and Henry Blackaby fill the shelves. It's a daunting task for any writer to jump into such a talented pool. Most of these writers mention the importance of a relationship with God, but I believe there will always be fresh insights available on this crucial topic. I hope I can offer some valuable insights.

Numerous books have been written about getting church right. Many books have been written about religion. But my goal is this book is to help the reader develop a closer relationship with God. I believe this is the very essence of Christianity.

The ideas in this book have evolved out of my personal ministry as I have moved from a church-based message to a relationship-based message. Like many preachers who were products of the sixties, I started out preaching religious forms and rules. I had rules for everything—rules for conversion, rules for church worship, rules for raising children, rules for a successful marriage, and general rules to live by. Life has tossed most of my rules out the window. They made good sermons, but terrible theology. As you will read in Chapter one, God is not about rules. The Pharisees were obsessed with rules. God loves us in spite of broken rules.

God wants men and women who have a relationship with Him. He wants real people who come to Him with real tears crying, "Father I have sinned again and broken your rules." "Create in me a pure heart, O God, and renew a steadfast spirit within me. Do not cast me from your presence or take your Holy Spirit from me. Restore to me the joy of your salvation" (Psalms 51:10-12).

God wants real people who don't brag to Him about how smart they were to find the right church, but pray confidently, "Even though I walk through the valley of the shadow of death, I will fear no evil, for you are with me" (Psalms 23:4). This beloved Psalm is about relationship. All the Psalms are about relationship. The whole Bible is about relationship. God forgive us if we have studied the Bible all our lives and missed this vital truth.

If you are living without a relationship with God, then you are not really living. I hope and pray that my book will help you in your journey toward a meaningful relationship with our God.

1

FINDING A RELATIONSHIP WITH GOD

I have taught college students for over three decades. I have discovered that some students will do the minimum to get by and I rarely remember their names. Other students stay and visit after class, drop by my office to chat, send frequent e-mails and even travel with me to professional conferences. I develop a relationship with these students. I not only know their names, but they become dear friends. Our relationship lasts long after the semester ends and years after they graduate from college. God's desire is to have a close relationship with His children, one that lasts long after this earthly life ends. Just like the student who builds a relationship with his teacher, we must make some effort to find a personal relationship with God.

Worship will be an empty ritual without a meaningful walk with God. Our young people will soon lose interest in religion unless they have a relationship with the God of the Bible. John wrote that Christians who walk with God have a special relationship with Him. "If we walk in the light, as he is in he light, we have fellowship with one another, and the blood of Jesus, his Son, purifies us from all sin" (I John 1:7). Only when we live in a relationship with God can we know the joy and security of our salvation.

Relationship is one of the sweetest words in our language. When we hear the word relationship we think of close friends, a close family, a marriage, or a close-knit congregation of believers. We think of our parents or married couples who have celebrated their golden wedding anniversary. The Greek word for relationship is *koinonia* which literally means "having in common." *Koinonia* is translated "fellowship" in the New Testament, but it was also used to describe the marriage relationship. *Koinonia* was the word used to describe a Christian's relationship with God as well as with other Christians. Just as a close-knit family has a lot in common, God and His children also have something in common—this spiritual fellowship is precious and wonderful. It is the highest good (the *summum bonum*) of the Christian's life.

Our Need for Connectedness

Everyone has heard the famous words written by John Donne in 1624, "No man is an island, entire of itself; every man is a piece of the continent, a part of the main."[1] Every person is connected to others through relationships. A quality life is made up of relationships and the highest relationship we have is our relationship with

God. Imagine how it would be to live in solitary confinement or to live on a deserted island all alone. Total isolation is not healthy emotionally or psychologically. Mankind yearns for connectedness to other human beings as well as to the God who made him. Today, many Christians go to church and study the Bible but don't feel close to God. They see God as a transcendent being who was active in Bible times but is not connected to their daily lives and problems. Add to this our contemporary urban life where people do not know their neighbors, even the residents of the apartment next to them. Many of us feel disconnected and alone in a world where no one cares. Peter urges his readers to "Cast your cares on him for he cares for you" (I Peter 5:7). Paul emphasized in Acts 17:27 that God is not far from every one of us. God knows the intimate details of our lives and listens to our prayers. Many traditional Christian hymns express the closeness we long for in our relationship with God: "Nearer My God to Thee, "I Come to the Garden Alone," and "My God and I."

Relationship Lost

In Genesis 3:8 God enjoyed walking and talking with Adam and Eve in the cool of the day. They were intimate friends and in the Garden of Eden there was no sickness, no sorrow, and no death. Adam and Eve and their descendents could have lived forever had it not been for the terrible curse of sin. God had a personal relationship with the patriarchs of old. Genesis tells us that Enoch "walked with God." God had a relationship with Noah, Abraham, Isaac, Joseph, and Moses. God's greatest desire is to have a relationship with His children. He sent Jesus to remove the blight of sin and restore relationship. Today, it is possible for sinful and imperfect people to walk with God just as Enoch did in the Old Testament. It is not only possible, it is normal. If you don't find an intimate, personal relationship with God, your spiritual life will be empty.

Sadly, a lot of people do not want a relationship with God. The story is told about an atheist who was in a boat with a friend drifting toward Niagara Falls. The atheist yelled in panic, "God help us."

The emergency passed and his friend asked, "Did I hear you calling out to God? I thought you were an atheist."

The atheist replied, "Atheism is OK under normal conditions but not when you are heading toward Niagara Falls!"

People can get through life without a relationship with God, but they have nothing to cling to in times of crisis.

One of the problems with church doctrine is that we tend to put all the emphasis on the process of conversion instead of relationship. My church tradition has put undue emphasis on baptism instead of relationship. We talk like getting baptized or "getting saved" is the high point of a Christian's life. It is not the high point but the beginning point. Conversion is not the end in itself but the means to the end. Many are baptized into Christ, which makes them part of God's family, but aren't aware of a personal relationship until years later, if ever. We allow God to forgive us but don't allow Him to adopt us as His children. God's children are not only a baptized people; they are "a relationship people."

A True Relationship

Many Christians practice religion but never develop a personal relationship with God. Karl Marx once said, "Religion is the opiate of the people."[2] Marx's brand of religion makes people feel good but it doesn't produce any life-changing results. Some Christians get caught up in religious legalism which is often mistaken for a real relationship with God. A biblical relationship with God is not "doing religion right" or following a set of rules. Families don't become close by following instruction manuals, but because of the relationship that binds them together. Even if some family members don't live praiseworthy lives, they still enjoy relationship because they are family.

God's view of righteousness is having an intimate relationship with Him. Abraham trusted God and walked by faith and his relationship was counted as righteousness even though he made some foolish mistakes in his life (Romans 4:3-24). David still had a relationship with God even though he broke a lot of rules. A relationship is more important than rules. Jesus told the Pharisees that they kept the rules but had no real relationship with the Father. Intimacy with God is not based on rules.

In Romans 3:23 Paul declares that "all have sinned and fallen short of the glory of God and are justified by his grace through the redemption that comes by Christ Jesus." How can we have a righteousness based on grace? Because Jesus came and died for our sins so we could be righteous and have a relationship with God. The gospel of Christ is not about performance but grace and relationship. Justification is God covering up for us because we have broken His rules. God wants an intimate relationship with us in spite of broken rules. When Jesus restores our relationship with God we no longer live to keep the rules, but are freed from the rules to know God and to love Him.

A relationship with God is not the same thing as going to church or attending Bible classes. I'm sure you've heard the old adage that sitting in a church will not make us Christians any more than sitting in a garage will make us cars. A relationship with God will bring us to church, but sitting in church will not necessarily give us a relationship with God. The Old Testament patriarchs offered sacrifices to God and lived lives of integrity, but did not spend time in church. Early Christians met for teaching, comfort, and communion during the apostolic era on the first day of the week (Acts 20:7). Still, some Christians, like the Ethiopian nobleman who was converted in Acts 8, returned to their homes and had no congregation of believers to meet with. These isolated Christians were still in fellowship with God because they were God's children. They didn't have the weekly encouragement of like-minded worshipers but they still had access to prayer and meditation. Joseph did not have any Jehovah worshipers to share his faith with in Egypt for over 90 years, but his relationship with God never wavered.

Only when our relationship with God transcends religious traditions and rituals, can we find true fulfillment. Only in an intimate relationship with God can forgiveness and grace be experienced. God loves us wholly and completely. Nothing else in life can offer us that. Only in a relationship with God does prayer become meaningful and personal. Only in a personal relationship with God do we learn the secret of total dependence on the one who protects and sustains us. An intimate relationship with God takes time and maturity. We may feel insecure at times and our prayers might seem clumsy and hesitant. But we were created in

God's image. We were created to communicate with Him, to speak to Him and listen to Him. We hear His voice in the Bible, but we also hear His voice in nature, in life's circumstances, and in the secret places of our hearts.

Religious leaders in first century Israel pointed people to religious rules. They were addicted to rules and religious rituals. Many people still have a problem with church rules and rituals today. According to a USA Today survey, 79% of people who do not attend church today say that Christianity is more about "organized religion" than about loving God and loving people.[3] Jesus pointed to a God who wanted a personal relationship with His people. Jesus taught that loving God and loving people were the two greatest commandments. The Pharisees focused on the law, but Jesus introduced us to the God of love who knows our hearts and offers us grace to cover our failures. Is it any wonder that the people who were most open-minded and receptive to Jesus were outcasts from the religious culture of their day—tax collectors, lepers, and prostitutes?

God has a plan for those who have a relationship with Him. His will is for us to walk hand-in-hand with Him through the journey of life. He doesn't promise everyone an easy journey. There will be tears and tragedies along the way. As I write these words it is Good Friday in Jerusalem. I am watching television as 100,000 Christian pilgrims walk the Via Dolorosa, the journey Jesus took to Golgotha. You don't have to follow the 14 "stations of the cross" to know that His journey was not easy, but for Jesus it was the way home.

Even as we journey "through the valley of the shadow of death," we will fear no evil when we have a relationship with God

(Psalms 23:4). He will lead us to our eternal home where our relationship will be closer and sweeter. Our relationship with God is forever.

1. Donne, John, Meditations XVII (indstate.edu/ilnprof/ENG451/ISLAND/index.html)

2. Marx, Karl (newsocialist.org/newsite/index.php)

3. Grossman, Kathy, "Survey: Non-attendees Find Faith Outside Church," USA Today, January 23, 2008 (www.USAToday.com/news/religion/2008-01-09-unchurched-survey)

1. What effort on our part does a relationship with God require?
2. What does a person have to do according to 1 John 1:7 to enjoy a relationship with God?
3. What is the Greek word for relationship? How is this word translated in most versions of the New Testament?
4. Why do we need relationships?
5. How might baptism be viewed as a means to an end rather than an end in and of itself?
6. What caused Adam and Eve to lose their relationship with God?
7. What is God's view of righteousness?
8. Is church attendance indicative of a relationship?
9. How was Jesus' emphasis different than the religious leaders of His day?
10. Why do the majority of people who do not attend church reject organized religion?

2

A PERSONAL RELATIONSHIP IS ENOUGH

I grew up singing work songs in the church such as "I Want to be a Worker for the Lord," "We'll Work Till Jesus Comes," and "Work For the Night is Coming." The purpose of these songs was to motivate Christians by making them feel they needed to do more work for the Lord. Yet many of the same Christians singing these songs were busy every night of the week with church activities. Some were involved in church to the neglect of their families. I suspect that many of the work songs grew out of a works-based salvation theology which came from Philippians 2:12 among other passages. In this Scripture, Paul tells us to "work out our salvation with fear and trembling." I heard a preacher say once that this passage scared him to death. A better understanding makes it less scary. The problem comes when verse 12 is separated from verse 13 which reads, "For it is God who works in you to will and to act according to his good purpose." Notice Who is doing the work in verse 13. It is God. This verse gives the reason for the fear and trembling. It is not because God will drop us into the fires of Hell if we don't work enough. It is because of the realization that the omnipotent God who created the universe is working in our lives to accomplish His purpose. Now that's scary. God is infinitely greater than we are and He will not give up. God has a purpose for every Christian, but it is not man's works that save us. Paul makes that clear in Ephesians 2:8, "For it is by grace you have been saved, through faith—and this not from yourselves, it is the gift of God— not by works, so that no one can boast."

It might be God's purpose that we win our spouse to Christ, or our boss, or co-worker, or neighbor, or friend. It is God's purpose that we bring our children up in the Lord. It might be God's purpose that we rise to a high position so we can stand for righteousness like Esther. It might be God's purpose that we become a prisoner like Paul. It might be God's purpose that we be martyred like Stephen or exiled like John. Whatever His purpose, it is God who is at work in us. It is not a salvation issue. It is a relationship issue.

I once heard an illustration about a man who died and met Peter at the gates of heaven. Peter explained to the man that he needed 1,000 points to enter. So the man began to list his accomplishments: "I was a Christian and went to church regularly."

"Good," said Peter, "That's one point."

"I also served as a deacon."

Peter replied, "That's another point."

"I was married to the same woman for 60 years."

"That's one more point."

Finally, the man got frustrated and exclaimed, "But for the grace of God, no one could enter heaven!"

"Excellent," said Peter. "That's 1,000 points."

It didn't take this man long to get the point. It's impossible to do enough works to get into heaven. It's all about relationship and grace.

I grew up thinking my good works were going to be placed on a set of scales and weighed against all the sins I have committed and the outcome would determine whether I was saved or lost. This scenario doesn't give Christians much confidence as they face their eternal destiny. I used to lie awake at night worrying because my sins were more numerous than my good works. The New Testament writers were much more positive about the confidence that comes from a relationship with God. Listen to these words of John: "I write these things to you who believe in the name of the Son of God so that you may *KNOW* that you have eternal life" (1 John 5:13). John did not say "that you may *hope* that you have eternal life." Knowledge is certainty and that certainty is based on God's grace.

Children have a relationship with their parents—a relationship based on love. As they become adults, that relationship grows and is not dependent on how much work they do or don't do. Some adult children cook and clean for an older parent who needs help - not to score points, but because they are family. If you have a relationship with God, everything you do is motivated by love. God's love for us is not based on the quality or quantity of our work. He loves all of

His children because we are family. We don't have to turn flips for God. He just wants to relate to us and to love us forever.

We need to let go of our guilt about working for the Lord. God loves us whether we read the Bible every day or not. He loves us whether we make a visit every day or not. He loves us whether we attend every church service or not. He loves us whether or not we mark a "daily Christian work" on our spiritual calendar. He loves us whether we do mission work in a foreign country or not. Many churches have a long list of activities members are encouraged to get involved in ranging from teaching Bible classes to Boy and Girl Scouts, vacation Bible school, blood drives, and Habitat for Humanity. These programs, while all are worthy, were set up by men not God.

Church leaders have tried to enforce faithfulness over the years with guilt inducing statements such as "only your best is good enough for God," "If you aren't doing all you can do for God, you should be ashamed," or "Jesus gave His all; nothing less than your all will please God."

Some will argue, God doesn't expect us to be lazy and do nothing in His kingdom. No, but God will give us opportunity if we will "bloom where we are planted." He will give us relationships in our neighborhoods and our workplace where we can be the voice and the hands of God. The Apostle Paul explains in Philippians 2:15 that when we live godly lives in a crooked and depraved generation, "we will shine as lights in the world." God does not want us to feel guilty. He just wants us to take the basket off and let our light shine where we are. Mother Teresa said she gave God permission to let Him touch others through her.[1] For over 45 years, she ministered to the poor, the sick, the orphaned, and the dying in her beloved city of Calcutta, India, while overseeing the Missionaries of Charity, which existed in over a hundred countries. We can't all be Mother Teresa. But we can all help somebody.

At the end of our lives, we will not be judged by how many diplomas we have, how much money we have made, how many honors we have won, or how many times we attended church. It all comes down to these simple words from the famous judgment scene described by Jesus: "I was hungry and you gave me something to eat, I was thirsty and you gave me something to drink, I was a stranger and you invited me in, I needed clothes and you clothed me, I was sick and you looked after me, I was in prison and you came to visit me" (Matthew 25:35-36). Every situation Jesus mentions is an opportunity to love someone, not a list we have to check off. All God wants is for us to represent Him on earth.

The Apostle Paul said our relationship with God can be summed up in one word—love. "Let no debt remain outstanding, except the continuing debt to love one another, for he who loves his fellowman has fulfilled the law. The commandments, Do not commit adultery, Do not murder, Do not steal, Do not covet, and whatever other commandments there may be are summed up in this one rule, love your neighbor as yourself" (Romans 13:8-9).

When Religion Becomes a Burden

When we follow a religion which consists of rules and laws, it becomes burdensome. Jesus condemned the Pharisees for their religious practices in Luke 11:46. "You load people down with burdens they can hardly carry and you yourselves will not lift a finger to help them." Paul warned about the evils of bad religion in Galatians 5:1. "It is for freedom that Christ has set us free. Stand firm, then, and do not let yourselves be burdened again by a yoke of slavery." Paul said Christ set us free from religion which consists of a set of rules. Many people today still bear the burden of religious legalism and guilt and they need to let go of these burdens. Paul wants us to have the freedom to simply have a personal relationship with God. Jesus, in Matthew 11:28-30, extended His great invitation to those who were struggling with heavy burdens in their lives. He said, "Come unto me all you who are weary and burdened, and I will give you rest. Take my yoke upon you and learn from me, for I am gentle and humble in heart, and you will find rest for your souls. For my yoke is easy and my burden is light." It was hard to keep all 613 laws in the Jewish Talmud, but it's easy to have a relationship with God. I grew up in a church of rules governing where you could go, what you should wear, how you should act, and how you should worship. There were more rules than you could possibly keep. This brand of religion is burdensome.

When we see the word "burden" in the words of Jesus and Paul we are quick to ascribe the reference to sin and corrupt living. But Paul was clearly talking about circumcision, a religious practice the Galatians were struggling with. Paul argued that we are free from religious burdens so we can be free to have a relationship with God. If you are still struggling with the burden of religion, you have missed out on the joy God wants you to have. You are trying so hard to be religious and pleasing to the church instead of just relaxing with the God who loves you and enjoying a relationship with Him.

James sums it up in James 1:27. "Religion that God our Father accepts as pure and faultless is this: to look after orphans and widows in their distress and to keep oneself from being polluted by the world." James does not mention how much doctrine you should know, how to worship, or how often to go to church. Benevolence and holiness come naturally when we have a relationship with God.

Micah, the Old Testament prophet, was struggling with this same religious question—how much is enough? Listen as the prophet asks, then answers a series of questions. "With what shall I come before the Lord and bow down before the exalted God? Shall I come before him with burnt offerings, with calves a year old? Will the Lord be pleased with thousands of rams, with ten thousand rivers of oil? Shall I offer my firstborn for my transgression, the fruit of my body for the sin of my soul? He has showed you O man, what is good. And what does the Lord require of you? To act justly, and to love mercy, and to walk humbly with your God" (Micah 6:6-8).

Justice, mercy, humility—these are the essence of a relationship with God. It's not what you do. It's who you are.

---

1. James Cardinal Hickey (www.ewtn.com/New_library/MT_hickey.htm)

1. How might attempting to "work your way into God's good graces" be an unhealthy approach?

2. How might we more effectively allow God to work in us and through us?

3. How does a healthy parent/child relationship show us the benefits of love over legalism?

4. What is the difference in personal laziness and feeling secure in God's grace?

5. What does God expect us to accomplish for Him?

6. When does religion become a burden to its followers?

7. Why do the prophet Micah's words give us comfort and confidence today?

SEVEN HABITS OF RELATIONSHIP PEOPLE

A relationship with God is difficult to describe in a few easy steps because every person's relationship is unique and personal. There are, however, some general characteristics that are common to all who enjoy a personal relationship with the Father. These characteristics will be summed up here and illustrated in chapters to follow.

Every relationship must have a beginning. Human relationships begin at birth when mother and family lovingly welcome their new addition. You could argue that a limited relationship exists prior to birth as the fetus moves inside the womb. But a full relationship is possible only when the baby becomes an independent person. Jesus explained to Nicodemus, "No one can see the kingdom of

God unless he is born again" (John 3:3). For a person to have a relationship with God, he must first be born again—cleansed by the blood of Christ, which washes away all sin. This initial cleansing occurs in conversion and continues to cleanse throughout the Christian's life (1 John 1:7).

A relationship with God takes time to develop and mature. It took Moses 40 years in the Arabian wilderness to learn total dependence on God. It took Saul of Tarsus three years in that same wilderness to develop his special relationship with God. A strong personal relationship with God is a continual process that is always developing and growing. It is not an event that happens at one point in time. A person does not have an intimate relationship at the point of conversion any more than a newborn has a mature relationship with his parents immediately after birth. A person doesn't receive a relationship with God through a vision or miraculous experience. Saul of Tarsus had both the vision and the miraculous experience that changed his life, but God knew he still needed a lot of training before he was ready to serve.

Habit # 1 - A person with a relationship with God has a constant awareness of God's presence 24 hours a day. Many Old Testament and New Testament characters who had that awareness were not major players in the Bible. In Genesis 16, we read about an Egyptian maidservant, Hagar, who became pregnant by Abraham and was driven away by Sarah's jealousy. The angel of the Lord spoke to Hagar when she stopped to rest by a spring in the desert. She was so overwhelmed by the realization that God knew who she was and where she was that she gave this name to God, "You are the

God who sees me" (Genesis 16:13). From that time on, Hagar had a constant awareness that God was present in her life.

God not only sees us but He promises to be with us. God told Moses, "Be strong and courageous. Do not be afraid or terrified because of them, for the Lord your God goes with you; he will never leave you nor forsake you" (Deuteronomy 31:6). When we are fully aware of God's presence in our daily lives, we will also recognize our total dependence on Him for every breath, for every heartbeat, for every bite of food, for every second of life, for the physical and spiritual strength needed for every circumstance in life.

Habit # 2 - A person who has a relationship with God loves God with all his heart, all his soul, and all his mind, which according to Jesus, is "the first and greatest commandment" (Matthew 22:37-39). Why does Jesus call this teaching the greatest commandment? Because a person who loves God with all his heart will gladly observe the rest of the commandments. When we are motivated by love, then we want to please God with all our being, not just follow a set of rules. When all our duties become our desires we are living the ideal life. John writes, "We love God because He first loved us" (1 John 4:19). The best soldier is one who loves his country. The true Christian is one who is motivated by love for God. Paul makes this argument in 1 Corinthians 13. "If I give all I possess to the poor and surrender my body to the flames, but have not love, I gain nothing."

Habit # 3 - A person with a right relationship with God is in communication with Him continually. God is the first person he speaks to upon waking up and the last person he speaks to when lying down at night. A relationship person talks to God throughout the day—before meals, in times of stress, in times of compassion, in times of meditation, in times of hurt, in times of fear, in times of joy, in times of concern, in times of temptation, in times of pain, in times of decision—the list could go on and on.

Communication with God also involves listening. God speaks to us through His revealed Word, but He also speaks to us through circumstances in our lives, through nature, and through the advice of spiritual friends. We need to develop an ear that is tuned to God.

Habit # 4 - A relationship with God motivates a person to seek out opportunities for spiritual growth and worship at church activities, seminars, camps, lectureships, television, the internet, DVD's, and books. Such a person "hungers and thirsts after righteousness" and his mind is set on spiritual things. A personal relationship causes one to spend quality time with God. A person with a strong relationship with God will make time for private meditation and prayer as well as form horizontal relationships with fellow believers who share their faith.

Habit # 5 - A person with a relationship with God radiates the Christian virtues contained in the Sermon on the Mount (humility, compassion, meekness, righteousness, mercy, purity, generosity, forgiveness, honesty) (Matthew 5-7), as well as the fruit of the Spirit (love, joy, peace, patience, kindness, goodness, faithfulness, gentleness, and self-control) (Galatians 5:22-23). This does not mean that a committed Christian is capable of living a perfect life. Jesus is the only one who lived a perfect life. But a person who has a personal relationship with God lives a transformed life. His life, though imperfect, is noticeably different because he has a higher set of priorities. Jesus asks us to "let your light shine before men that they may see your good deeds and praise your Father in heaven" (Matthew 5:16).

Habit # 6 - A relationship with God will produce the "mind of Christ" (Philippians 2:5 KJV). In this Scripture, Paul is referring to the humility of Christ who willingly became a servant in order to accomplish God's will on earth. Star Trek fans are familiar with the term "mind meld" when two minds literally are fused together as one. Only when a Christian's mind is fused together with the mind of Christ does he become Christ-minded. This means that he thinks like Christ, speaks like Christ, acts like Christ, and seeks God's will in every aspect of his life.

Habit # 7 - A relationship with God produces a healthy confidence in the grace of God and the security of your eternal salvation. John wrote his first epistle so that Christians might *know* that they have eternal life (1 John 5:13). John used the word "know" no less than 41 times in his letters and yet some Christians still live with a question mark in their lives instead of an explanation point. I have visited many terminally ill Christians who continued to use "if" statements to their dying breath. "If the good Lord forgives me," "If I've been found worthy," and "If I get to heaven." These statements cause me great sadness as I think about how a theology of rules and a works-based salvation has stolen the hope and joy from the hearts of many of God's children. John wrote, "Dear children, continue in him so that when he appears we may be confident and unashamed before him at his coming" (1 John 2:28). Our confidence is not based on our own righteousness but on our relationship with God. Confidence is not wrong when it is based on the sufficiency of Christ's cleansing blood and the assurance of God's amazing grace toward His beloved children.

1. When does your relationship with God begin?
2. When does your relationship with God reach its peak in your life?
3. What difference does a constant awareness of God's presence make in a Christian's life?
4. Why does Jesus say that loving God is the first and greatest commandment?
5. How does a person who has a relationship with God communicate with Him?
6. What opportunities for spiritual growth can you think of which are not mentioned in this chapter?
7. How can a human being have the "mind of Christ?"
8. On what basis can a Christian have a certainty of his eternal salvation?

4

THE GOD WHO SEEKS RELATIONSHIP

The God of the Bible seeks a relationship with people created in His image. God initiated relationships in the Bible with individuals who were in prison and were in times of crisis. He spoke from a burning bush, sometimes He roared like thunder, other times He spoke with a "gentle whisper." I believe God still moves to initiate relationships today with people who are receptive to Him. God's relationship with us is not based on our goodness or performance but on our faith that He loves us, that He wants to help us, and that we are important to Him. Undoubtedly, some of the individuals God reached out to did not have an accurate concept of God until much later in their lives.

Four Views of God

Most Americans believe in God, but they picture God in very different ways. According to Paul Froese and Christopher Bader, sociologists at Baylor University, defined four views of God in their 2007 research.[1] First, is the "authoritarian God" who is engaged in human events and metes out punishment in this life to those who do not follow Him. This view is held by 28 percent, the largest group of Americans. The second view is the "benevolent God," shared by 22 percent of Americans, who loves everyone and supports us in caring for the needy. The third view sees God as a "critical God" who keeps an eye on this world, is grieved by human suffering, and delivers harsh justice in the next world. This view is held by 21 percent. The fourth concept the authors call the "distant God," a view held by about a fourth (24 percent) of American believers. This view sees a God who booted up the universe and then left us on our own. The "distant God" concept is more prevalent in Europe than America. Buddhism and Hinduism are examples of this type of deity. Five percent of the 1,648 people surveyed were atheists. The sample used in the study reflected the typical American public.

It is unfortunate that the researchers selected negative terms to describe God. The terms authoritarian, critical, and distant have a negative connotation whether you are describing God or a parent. I think of a police officer as authoritarian, a domineering mother as critical, and the president as distant, but these terms do not come to mind when describing the God I know. Many visualize the God of the Old Testament as more authoritarian because He punished His people directly for their disobedience and made numerous references to His wrath. The New Testament reveals a benevolent

God who loves us and does us good all the days of our lives. He allows suffering in this life, but the suffering is not punishment for how a person has lived. God is not waiting to zap people every time they mess up. God sent His Son as an expression of His grace toward us.

Inadequate Concepts of God

Many years ago J. B. Phillips wrote a provocative book entitled, Your God Is Too Small, in which he claimed that many people have an inadequate concept of God.[2] Some think of God as an old grandfather who sits in a rocking chair in heaven with a long, white beard. Some think God is only their conscience or a domineering parent who enjoys telling them what to do. Some think God is a crutch for the weak—a god of the sick, helpless, and elderly. Others think of God as simply a powerful machine like a giant computer that created the world but is not involved in its day-to-day operation. To some people, God is only a genie in a lamp who appears when they get in trouble. They make a 911 call to God only when they need help.

Perhaps the worst concept of God is a second-hand God. Many people who were raised in religious homes simply adopt the god of their parents or grandparents. Some merely accept the god of their church, their friends, or their youth group and have no real personal relationship with God. They have never studied, prayed, or trusted in God for themselves. The true God cannot be handed down like a family Bible or a set of china. God has no grandchildren.

People cannot have a mature relationship with God if they still hold to a child's concept of the supreme deity. They can't continue to worship the same concept of God they had as a child. When my son was small, we would occasionally get our t-shirts mixed up in the laundry and I could not pull his over my head. The same is true when spiritual knowledge doesn't keep up with secular knowledge. Scientific knowledge and technological knowledge doubles every five years. When people spend no time studying God's revelation and their faith fails to grow and mature, it's no wonder their concept of God remains childlike.

The Nature of God

1. *The God of the Bible is Spirit.* Jesus explained in John 4:24 that "God is spirit and his worshipers must worship in spirit and in truth." Sometimes people make the mistake of thinking God is like man—with the same limitations and weaknesses human beings have. Occasionally Bible writers give God human attributes such as a face, hands, heart, eyes, ears, and mouth. These figures of language are called anthropomorphisms that help the reader relate to an invisible God. But the true God has no physical form. He is pure intelligence, pure energy, and pure personality.

2. *God almighty is sovereign.* He has the divine right to do as He chooses, for He answers to no one. God is omnipotent which means "all-powerful." Jesus said, "Nothing is impossible with God" (Luke 1:37). God is never puzzled or disturbed at earthly events for His purposes are always accomplished even in the worst human tragedies.

3. *The God of the Bible is omniscient.* He knows everything—past, present, and future. His knowledge is eternal, infinite, and limitless.

His "all-seeing eye" follows us every moment of our lives. God is omnipresent and his presence fills the heavens and the earth. The Psalmist concluded "Such knowledge is too wonderful for me, too lofty for me to attain. Where can I go from your Spirit? Where can I free from your presence?" (Psalms 139:6,7).

4. *God is majestic.* The Bible makes numerous references to God's splendor, glory, and majesty. Isaiah saw the Lord seated on a throne, high and exalted and the train of his robe filled the temple. Above him were seraphs calling to another, "Holy, holy, holy is the Lord Almighty; the whole earth is full of his glory." At the sound of their voices, the posts and thresholds shook and the temple was filled with smoke (Isaiah 6:1-4). The Psalmist wrote, "The Lord reigns, He is robed in majesty. The Lord is robed in majesty and is armed with strength. The world is firmly established; it cannot be moved" (Psalms 93:1). We can still see His majesty in creation as we are awed by snow capped mountains, the ocean, or the stars.

5. *God is the essence of love.* John, the Apostle of love, tell us repeatedly that "God is love" (1 John 4:8). God's love can be seen in His relationship with His people throughout the Bible. John says God's love can best be seen in the sacrifice of His precious Son for man's sins and that God's loving spirit will be evident in all who have a relationship with Him. Jesus says God's love can be compared to the father's love in the parable of the prodigal son in Luke 15. The son wasted his inheritance with wild living and irresponsibility, but his father was lovingly, anxiously awaiting his return and forgave him with great joy. God loves us so much He will use every possible means to bring us home and shower us with blessings. God's love is relentless—He will follow us to the ends of the earth and never stop loving us.

6. *God is holy.* He has said, "I am the Lord your God; consecrate yourselves and be holy because I am holy" (Leviticus 11:44). Holy means pure, set apart from all wickedness and corruption. God is completely wholesome, perfect and incapable of evil. This often makes God appear transcendent, far above the sin and imperfection of mankind. Jesus, God's Son, came to earth to bridge the gap and show men how they could also be holy through His blood.

7. *God is just.* God is faithful to His word and His judgment is righteous and perfect. On the surface, this trait of God seems inconsistent with God's love. How can God love everyone and yet be perfect in His judgment? How can a loving God condemn the unrighteous to eternal punishment? The answer is that God is not honorable unless He is fair. God would not be fair unless He rewarded the righteous and punished the unrighteous as He promised. He sent Jesus to make it possible for all sinners to become righteous through His sacrifice.

8. *God is gracious and merciful toward those who embrace Him.* God's grace refers to His unmerited favor and good will toward men. Mercy refers to forgiveness, kindness, or the withholding of punishment that is due. God's grace and mercy are dual themes that run throughout the Bible. "The Lord is merciful and gracious, slow to anger. For as the heaven are high above the earth, so great is his mercy toward those who fear him" (Psalms 103:8,11 KJV). God forgives all of a believer's sins (mercy) when one accepts Christ who is God's gift of grace to the world. God's forgiveness continues to bless the lives of those who have a relationship with Him. "His compassions never fail. They are new every morning. Great is his faithfulness" (Lamentations 3:22,23). Salvation is a free gift which is not earned or deserved by human works. Eternal life is also a gift of grace which God has promised to all His children. Since heaven is based on grace not works, all who have a personal relationship with God enjoy the blessed assurance of eternal life.

9. *God is eternal.* He has no beginning and no end. He has always existed and always will. He does not need man to exist and is not dependent on man to love Him. He could have created and terminated many worlds and universes such as ours. What was God doing before our world began in Genesis one? Our finite minds are incapable of comprehending the infinity of God. Moses said it best, "From everlasting to everlasting Thou art God" (Psalms 90:2 KJV).

In His Image

"So God created man in his own image; in the image of God he created him" (Genesis 1:27). What did God mean by the word "image"? God did not say that He created any of the animals in His image. Many people have mistakenly inferred that God was talking about His physical image—eyes, ears, arms, legs, and heart. If so, then apes, monkeys, bears, and kangaroos would also be in God's image because they all share these physical characteristics.

We can look at these nine characteristics of God and get a good idea about what God meant by "his own image." God is a living spirit and "breathed into man's nostrils and man became a living soul." God is eternal and He imparted to man a portion of His own eternalness. Every person has within him a spark of deity—

a never dying soul that is in God's image. God is sovereign and gives human beings sovereign control of their own soul. We have the opportunity to choose whether to follow God or reject God. He gives us the freedom of choice over our own eternal destiny. God is all-intelligent and He gave mankind a supreme intelligence above all creatures on the earth. He gave man the mental power to "rule over the fish of the sea, the birds of the air, the livestock, the creatures that move along the ground, and over all the earth" (Genesis 1: 26). Likewise, God gave man the unique capacity to love, to be holy, to be just, and to be merciful.

People who have a personal relationship with God become more and more like God. As Christians seek to become more like Christ whom God sent to be our model, we become more like the Father. We can't have a meaningful relationship with someone unless we have some similarities. Amos, the prophet, asked, "How can two walk together except they be agreed?" (Amos 3:3)

The God who knew us before we were conceived, who knows our every thought and every desire, who knows our every weakness and every failure, wants to have a relationship with us. That is an awesome concept. No wonder the Psalmist exclaimed, "Such knowledge is too wonderful for me, too lofty for me to attain" (Psalms 139:6).

1. Froese, Paul, and Bader, Christopher, <u>America's Four Gods: What We Say About God And What That Says About Us</u>, Oxford University Press, 2010, p. 176.

2. Phillips, <u>J. B. Your God Is Too Small,</u> New York, Macmillan, 1964.

1. Which of the four views of God best fits your current personal view?

2. Is there a difference in the Old Testament God and the New Testament God? Explain your answer.

3. What childish concepts of God did you grow up with?

4. What is the difference between God being authoritarian and God being sovereign?

5. What is the difference between God being critical and God being just?

6. How can God be loving and gracious and still condemn souls to eternal punishment?

7. If God is omniscient and knows events ahead of time, how can He let bad things happen to good people?

8. What does it mean to be created in God's image?

9. How can we become more like God?

5

A PERSONAL WALK WITH GOD

"Enoch walked with God" (Genesis 5:24). What a wonderful epitaph for a man's life. We don't know much about Enoch, except that he was the father of Methuselah, the oldest man in the Bible. But this description speaks volumes. In a society of great wickedness, Enoch had a personal relationship with God. Jude 14 says he was a prophet, a preacher of righteousness. An ancient Arab legend claims Enoch was the father of writing. Wouldn't you love to know what a typical day in Enoch's life was like or how often he spoke with God? Enoch was contemporary with Adam and lived long before written Scripture. He had a relationship with God without ever reading the Bible or being a member of a synagogue or church. Enoch was taken up to heaven where he continues to enjoy that relationship for eternity.

A child once explained Enoch's story this way. "Enoch had walked with God a long way when evening came. Enoch asked God to go back home with him for the night. God said, 'My house is closer' and took Enoch to his home in heaven. Enoch was so happy there that he stayed and never returned to earth." What a wonderful story about a special relationship.

Adam and Eve also had a unique relationship with God. God spoke directly to them and made their first articles of clothing. Adam and Eve were enticed by Satan to sin just as God's children are today, but God doesn't stop loving us.

Noah walked with God for nearly a thousand years. Genesis 6:8 says, "Noah was a righteous man, blameless among the people of his time and he walked with God." Noah's obedience is legendary even though the ark took over a century to build. Noah was 600 years old when the promised flood came and his relationship with God saved his and his family's lives.

Abraham had a relationship with God that caused him to move to an unknown land simply on his faith in God's promise. Abraham made mistakes and did not live a perfect life, but God made him the father of the Jewish nation. Abraham's great-grandson, Joseph, also had a personal relationship with God that sustained him through the trials of slavery, betrayal and imprisonment. Joseph's relationship with God can be seen in his forgiveness, love, and grace toward his treacherous brothers. Joseph lived 110 years in a trusting relationship with God.

Job had a relationship with God that gave him unshakable faith even in agonizing suffering. Job spoke to God and God responded.

He walked with God all the days of his life and was blessed abundantly after his suffering had ended. Job's life is a beautiful illustration of the Psalm that says, "Weeping may endure for a night but joy comes in the morning" (Psalms 30:5).

Moses' relationship with God is well-known. He was a child of privilege but the riches of Pharaoh could not destroy his unfaltering relationship. For 40 years he led three million people through the wilderness to accomplish God's will. What an intimate relationship this great man had.

King David stands out as a "man after God's own heart" (1 Samuel 13:14). The Psalms give us an intimate glimpse into his personal relationship with God. David, during his reign, drifted into polygamy, adultery, and murder but he always turned to God in penitence and prayer.

If one had asked Saul of Tarsus, persecutor of Jewish heretics, if he had a relationship with God, he would have answered with a definite yes. The problem was that Saul's relationship was one-sided. He mistook zeal and legalism for a relationship. He mistook theological training and observance of religious ceremonies as a relationship.

He also mistook the esteem and praise of men (the Pharisees) as a relationship. Many people today make the same mistakes. God took Saul's superficial relationship and made it a real relationship based on the blood of Christ His Son. Saul spent three years in the wilderness of Arabia learning how to communicate with God (Galatians 1:7). Paul also learned total dependence—God supplied his food and sustenance. Paul learned that true fellowship with God could not be found in synagogues, temples, and churches. It could not be found in the rabbinical schools or universities. A true relationship is found in knowing Jesus and spending time alone with God.

What Did They Have in Common?

Looking back over these examples from the Bible, there are common threads running through their lives. First, they all communicated with God. They spoke to God and He spoke to them in various ways. Second, they were all men of faith. They trusted in God even though they often suffered great adversity. Hebrews chapter 11 honors these men and others because of their outstanding faith. Third, these men demonstrated a total dependence on God which takes extreme humility. Moses could never have divided the Red Sea or fed the Israelites for 40 years without total dependence on God. Finally, they all had a constant awareness of God's presence. For Moses, God's presence was a pillar of cloud by day and a pillar of fire by night. Ancient tradition says during Potiphar's wife's attempt to seduce Joseph, she threw a covering over a statue of an Egyptian god and said, "Now God can't see us." Joseph replied, "My God always sees."

Most of the men described above, lived before formal religious systems were established. In fact, after the temple was built religious ceremonies began to take precedence over a personal relationship with God. The prophets decried the apathy which developed among the Jews. Many worshipers would bring their annual sacrifice to the altar and never think about God until next year's Passover. Their personal ethics and family life were often no different than the pagans who surrounded them. In fact, idolatry, divorce, dishonesty, and debauchery were commonplace among God's people even in the heart of Judea.

Relationship Is Individual

A personal relationship with God must be lived on an individual basis. God does not promise to save family units, congregations, churches, or nations today. He saves individual believers through Christ. Holiness is an individual matter. It's not enough to have holy parents, holy siblings, holy ancestors, or belong to a holy church. It's helpful if your spouse has a personal relationship with God, but it doesn't make up for your lack of one. Holiness starts in one's heart. Holiness doesn't start with externals but with internals. Holiness is not a set of rules and regulations but a relationship of trust and total surrender to God.

Worship is also an individual endeavor. We talk about corporate worship. But just because hundreds of people are sitting in a sanctuary while worship takes place does not mean that every person is worshiping from his heart.

The story is told of a soul in heaven who was escorted by an angel on a visit back to earth. They observed a church singing hymns, but heard no sound. Finally, they heard the voice of one small girl singing, "My Jesus I Love Thee."

The angel explained, "You are hearing worship as God hears it—the only person in this church who is singing from her heart at this moment is that little girl."

The Christian disciplines—dedication, prayer, Bible study, meditation, and fasting must grow out of an individual relationship with God. In the final judgment, every person will stand before

God individually. Paul writes, "for we must all appear before the judgment seat of Christ that each one may receive what is due him for the things done while in the body whether good or bad" (2 Corinthians 5:10).

Bible examples as well as the individual nature of Christianity suggest that it is possible for individuals to have a personal relationship with God and never be connected to an organized church with a name on its door. Yes, God adds us to His "universal church family" when we are saved (Acts 2:41), but we may not get to know many of our spiritual family on earth. The thief on the cross didn't get a chance to celebrate with any of his earthly brothers and sisters. It is possible for a believer to be a "Christian only" without involvement in a religious organization. This is not the ideal, however, because Christ's Apostles established local congregations and recognized that Christians grow better in a nurturing environment. But it is possible that one could live in a geographical area where a family of worshipers does not exist. Some people lack transportation or are homebound because of a disability. I have known Christians with agoraphobia that could not assemble with a crowd of people. What about lepers in the first century? Many of them believed but were not allowed in the church or even the city because they were unclean. What about natives in the jungle, hermits, homeless, prisoners, and soldiers in remote places who believe but are isolated from any congregation or formal religion? I have assisted homeless believers in baptism who had no address, no identification, no transportation, and never returned to church again that I knew of. Think about the converts from World Bible School who learn the gospel via correspondence

A Relationship With God

courses and have no place to worship. If these people can't be saved based on their relationship with God alone, then why do we bother to evangelize them in the first place?

Picture in your mind a believer who lives on a deserted island—no organized church, no Christian friends around, no communication, no worship services or Bible classes. You have just pictured the aged Apostle John who wrote, "I am in the spirit on the Lord's Day" while on the Island of Patmos where he was exiled for life (although church historians say he was ultimately brought back and died in the city of Ephesus) (Revelation 1:10). John was prevented from practicing his religion or participating in church which was why he was exiled in the first place—an attempt by Roman authorities to rid the Christian religion of its leaders.

Consider another example. In Acts 8 we read the story of the conversion of an official from Ethiopia who learned about salvation in Christ from Philip, the evangelist, while riding in his chariot on the way back home. The Ethiopian had a relationship with God because he had been to Jerusalem to worship as a Jewish proselyte. But his relationship was not complete in Christ until he learned of the Messiah and was baptized into his saving blood. As he returned home however, he returned to a country with no church or Christians as far as we know. We like to fantasize that he, in time, converted others to join him and formed a church, but there is no evidence that he did or even was allowed to evangelize in Ethiopia which probably had its own religious culture. Suppose this Christian man lived the rest of his life and never had the opportunity to enjoy a worship service or the Lord's supper with other Christians. What if he never had the chance to learn a Christian hymn or read from an inspired Christian writer? Would anyone dare say it was impossible for this man to go to heaven because he never went to church and never took communion? He had a personal relationship with God but he might never have been known in the Queen's court as a "religious man."

I have known believers, who had a relationship with God, but stayed away because the local church was fighting and destroying one another over petty issues, filled with hatred, or polluted with sacrilegious practices in the name of worship. I have known believers who have been deeply wounded by the local church and been told they are unwelcome. Perhaps one stays home because of terrorism or persecution. Some believers have been excluded from an organized church because of racism, homophobia, or prejudice of another kind. Will we limit God's grace and say these people cannot go to heaven because they were not active members of a church and did not attend regular religious services?

A personal relationship with God means that I, as an individual, can commune with God anywhere at anytime. My own relationship with God has never been stronger than on camping trips around the campfire at night, on the top of a mountain or on a boat in the moonlight. God appreciates and accepts our worship from our camper or beside the campfire. Some of the most effective worship services I have engaged in were in motel rooms in distant cities with family or college students with whom I was traveling.

A Christian is the "temple of the Holy Spirit" (1 Corinthians 6:19). He doesn't have to get in a car or bus to find a temple in which to worship. A Christian is his own "priest." (1 Peter 2:9) He doesn't have to go find a priest or cathedral to validate his worship.

Every Christian is a walking, talking temple of the Lord. Although Christians derive many benefits from corporate worship, God cannot be confined to church buildings and structures made with human hands. Paul made this clear in Acts 17:24. God communicated with Adam and Eve in the garden, with Hagar in the desert, with Joseph in prison, with Moses in a burning bush, with the Apostles in a stormy sea, and with Jesus on top of a mountain. Psalms 145 declares, "The Lord is near to all who call on him; to all who call upon him in truth. He fulfills the desires of those who fear him; he hears their cry and saves them. The Lord watches over all who love him" (Psalms 145:18-19).

1. Why does Enoch's relationship with God stand out in the Bible?

2. How did Noah demonstrate his relationship with God?

3. What did Abraham's life show about his relationship with God?

4. How did you know Joseph had a strong relationship with God?

5. Explain how Saul of Tarsus changed from a wrong relationship to a right relationship with God?

6. Other than those mentioned in this chapter, what Bible examples can you think of that had a personal relationship with God?

7. Explain why our relationship with God must be individual in nature. If the goal is an individual, personal relationship with God, why do we have church fellowship?

8. Give situations where it might be possible for a person could have a relationship with God and not attend regular church services.

9. Did the Ethiopian nobleman have a church in his native country? How might he have built his relationship with God without a family of believers?

10. What does it mean to be the "temple of the Holy Spirit"?

6

RELIGION AND RELATIONSHIP

Many years ago I read a story about the captain of a whaling vessel in the North Atlantic who saw, through his binoculars, an indistinct hulk in the distance surrounded by icebergs. As his ship came near he called, "Ship ahoy" but received no answer. Upon boarding the vessel he found a frozen captain and crew. The captain was fully dressed sitting at his desk before an open log book. The last entry revealed that the ship had been drifting for 10 years. It was a floating sepulcher, tossed by the wind and the waves, drifting from no port to no port. This ship is a fitting illustration of many religious people who, on the surface, appear to be devout but inside have no spiritual life. They are religious people who go through the motions, but have no viable relationship with God.

Many people practice a form of religion. They attend a church and participate in the rituals and sacraments observed by that religious institution. Many attend service every Sunday, but walk out the doors of the church and don't think about God until the next service. Some go to church services for all the wrong reasons. One might go to church just to please his parents or a spouse. Another may attend to see friends. Still others go to show off their clothes, cars, or babies. Some attend church for food, movies, or entertainment.

Even worse, many Christians exit the church services and take the Lord's name in vain, lie, cheat, steal, abuse alcohol and drugs, abuse their spouses and children, and live a sinful, materialistic life week after week. Some of the greatest criminals down through history have been religious people. Even Adolf Hitler was religious as a boy, singing in the choir and planning to be a priest. In the familiar words of the African-American preacher, "Many people talk the talk, but don't walk the walk." We sometimes call them hypocrites. Sometimes we call them brothers. Sometimes we call them elders or preachers. The number of high-profile televangelists and priests in America who in recent years have been found guilty of sexual or financial shenanigans is troubling.

In Acts 17, Paul entered Athens and couldn't help but notice the statues of Greek gods and goddesses around the various temples. His first words were, "Men of Athens; I see that in every way you are very religious" (Acts 17:22). Some took this as a compliment until he told them about the true God who raised His Son from the dead. The Athenians are an example of people who had a form of religion, but no relationship with God.

A religious person without a relationship with God is not necessarily a bad person—just a Christian living an empty life. Like the ghost ship in the opening paragraph, they look good sitting in church on Sunday, but inside they are spiritually dead. Like artificial flowers they look pretty until a closer examination reveals they are not real. The Pharisees of Jesus' day were a prime example of people who were religious in their worship and Sabbath rituals, but lacked a real relationship with God. Jesus said, "They honor me with their lips, but their hearts are far from me. They worship me in vain because their teachings are but rules taught by men" (Matthew 15:8). The Pharisees are an example of people who had religion, but not a relationship with God. Judas Iscariot (Matthew 26:13) and Ananias and Saphira (Acts 5) are examples of New Testament believers who had religion but lacked a proper relationship with God.

A Living Sacrifice

The problem with many religious people is that mentally they compartmentalize their lives. Their lives are like a pie cut into eight pieces. They give God one piece of the pie and give the other pieces to their families, jobs, recreation, travel, civic duties, rest, and other endeavors. This person's life is 7/8 secular and 1/8 religious. Christians who have a genuine relationship with God are much more than just 1/8 religious or even 1/2 religious. Relationship people are one-hundred percent religious. God does not want one piece of the pie. The whole pie belongs to Him.

Paul, in Romans 12:1, gives a unique description of a Christian's life: "Offer your bodies as living sacrifices, holy and pleasing to

God—this is your spiritual act of worship." This was a radically new concept to the believers at Rome. They were accustomed to animal sacrifices in which animals were killed at the altar. The sacrificial animal was offered totally to God. If a Christian's body is offered as a living sacrifice then everything he does in his body is offered to God. One-hundred percent of his life is dedicated to God and everything he does in that body is holy. Only when a Christian becomes fully aware of this essential truth can he truly walk with God.

The biggest reason why many of us end up with religion instead of a relationship with God is that most churches are preoccupied with getting religious forms and rituals right. The church I grew up in was notorious for emphasizing religion instead of relationship. In other words, we spent most of our church time teaching about the proper acts of public worship, theological issues, and church doctrines. Preachers were fond of preaching against the sins of wrong living (smoking, drinking, drugs, etc.). Sadly, I cannot remember a single sermon on developing an intimate relationship with God.

Christians who participate in corporate worship and church activities are well-meaning people. They believe the church is important and every religious form has value. They are opposed to the removal of the Bible and prayer from the public schools and public events. They fail to realize that people who have a relationship with God pray continually (1 Thessalonians 5:17). No court, no security guard, no police force can prevent God's children from praying in a school bus, classroom, ball game, concert, or courtroom.

Religion Without Relationship

Religion without relationship was a serious problem in the first century church as it is today. John, in his New Testament letters, battled the dualism doctrine taught by the Gnostics in the churches of Asia. These heretics claimed that as long as you went to church and fed your soul, it didn't matter how you lived in the flesh. They believed that the body could do as it pleased (fornication, drunkenness, and all forms of debauchery) and it would not affect the spiritual part of a man. John wrote, "Dear children, do not let anyone lead you astray. He who does what is right is righteous just as he is righteous. He who does what is sinful is of the devil, because the devil has been sinning from the beginning. The reason the Son of God appeared was to destroy the devil's work. No one who is born of God will continue to sin, because God's seed remains in him; he cannot go on sinning, because he has been born of God" (1 John 3:7-9).

Religion without relationship is the most dangerous condition in the world. It gives many people a false sense of security. It fosters the following attitudes: "I am a church-goer, I can do anything I want to and it's OK." "I have been saved by God's grace. What need do I have of prayer, meditation, and Bible study?" "I know it's wrong, but I went to church Sunday—that should take care of it."

Religion without relationship is what led to the doctrine of absolution to which Martin Luther protested so courageously in the Middle Ages. Absolution is where one can perform a religious ritual or pay a sum of money to have your sin absolved. The obvious extension of this doctrine is that you can ask for absolution in advance (purchase what the church aptly called "indulgences") and feel free to commit the sin because you have already "paid for it." Practices such as this make a mockery of true religion. A Christian who has a right relationship with God does not want to commit sin and realizes that only true penitence will bring God's forgiveness.

Religion without a relationship with God is false religion. It gives the illusion that one is spiritually sound when the opposite is true. This kind of religion is shallow, superficial, and unsatisfying. It is a church-based exercise instead of a God-based lifestyle. It creates fake Christians instead of genuine Christians. James, the brother of Jesus, wrote, "Religion that God our Father accepts as pure and faultless is this: to look after orphans and widows in their distress and to keep oneself from being polluted by the world" (James 1:27). God is not satisfied with anything less than a pure, personal, day-to-day relationship with his children. We need to drop the baggage of religion and "churchianity" and just be Christians only.

Obstacles to a Relationship With God

There is an illustration about a conversation between Satan and his angels. He said, "We can't keep Christians from going to church; we can't keep them from reading their Bibles; we can't stop them from living good lives; but one thing we can do is steal their time so they can't develop a meaningful relationship with God." So the evil angels went eagerly to their task causing Christians everywhere to get busier and more rushed for time. Has Satan been successful at his scheme? You be the judge.

This illustration makes a good point. *One of the obstacles to a right relationship with God is the busy lifestyle we lead in today's society.* I can't imagine Enoch distracted by TV, cell phones, newspapers, internet, music lessons, sporting events, and pressures of the workplace. Enoch lived in an uncomplicated world—a world in which he had time for God daily. Yes, he lived in a world corrupted by sin, but he found times to get away and meet God in the garden or on the mountain top where he could communicate with God without distraction. We need to create sacred times to be alone with God away from the cell phones and beepers.

Another obstacle to a relationship with God is that we often substitute "going to church" for a personal relationship. A healthy relationship stays in touch "24/7." God is in our thoughts, our plans, our prayers, and our very consciousness. Some Christians have no relationship with God outside of church. This problem has led many to "lose their religion" when they go off to college or to a military assignment away from home. God had a relationship with His people long before He brought the church into existence. Enoch, Noah, and Abraham had a relationship with God long before the Law of Moses with its tabernacle and religious protocol.

A third reason why many do not enjoy a relationship with God is sin. Isaiah 59:2. describes such people. "Your iniquities have separated between you and God, and your sins have hid his face from you that he will not hear." Jesus died to remove the curse of sin from people's lives. Yet, if a believer continues to persist in a conscious, deliberate sin, knowing it violates God's will and grieves the Spirit, it not only hinders his prayer life but interferes with a right relationship with God.

A fourth obstacle to a relationship with God is pride. God warns in the Proverbs that, "Pride goes before destruction" (Proverbs 16:18) and "I hate pride and arrogance" (Proverbs 8:13).

Pride is a human feeling that affects us all at one time or another. Moses was struck by pride when he failed to give God credit for producing water from the rock. Peter was overcome with pride when he promised he would never forsake Jesus, but later denied him three times. Sometimes pride creeps into our lives in subtle ways. We start feeling proud of what we have accomplished or proud of our family or proud of our material possessions. The problem is that pride leaves God out of the picture.

A fifth obstacle is human selfishness. Selfishness, like pride, puts "me" first instead of God. Jesus told a parable about a selfish farmer whose crops were so plentiful that he tore down his old barns and built bigger ones. He never thought about sharing his blessings with his neighbors and those less fortunate. Jesus said to the farmer, "You fool. This night your soul will be demanded from you. Then you will get what you have prepared for yourself" (Luke 12:16-20). Selfish people never think about anyone but themselves. They have no room for God in their lives.

God still wants to have a relationship with us in spite of the obstacles we erect in His way. His love is relentless and He will not give up on us. God is reaching out to us today and we can continue to put up obstacles or we can open our hearts and share our lives with the God who wants to walk through life with us.

A Relationship With God

1. What are some signs that a person might be religious and have no relationship with God?

2. What does it mean to "offer your bodies as living sacrifices"?

3. What evidence do you find that religion without relationship was a problem in the first century?

4. How can we drop the baggage of religion and just be "Christians only"?

5. How might our busyness interfere with our relationship with God?

6. Give examples of how pride and selfishness can destroy an effective relationship with God.

7. How does God still pursue a relationship with us when we have erected obstacles in His way?

7

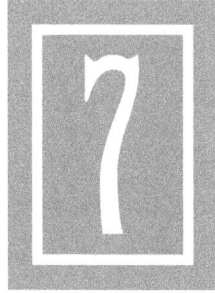

THE SPIRIT'S FIRE — PROOF OF RELATIONSHIP

I love the story of the two taxidermists who stopped in front of a window where a horned owl was on display. They immediately began to criticize the workmanship. "Its eyes are not natural." "Its wings aren't exactly right." "His head and feathers are not arranged neatly." "The feet could be improved." All of a sudden, the owl winked at them. It was alive!

This story reminds me of all who criticize the different beliefs concerning the Holy Spirit. Some are quick to criticize the "holy rollers," the "shakers," the "charismatics," the "faith healers," and everyone else whose practice differs from theirs, but they sometimes overlook one overwhelming and frightening truth—the Holy Spirit is alive! The Holy Spirit is real and alive in God's people whether we agree or disagree on the proper signs and manifestations.

People with a personal relationship with God are possessed by a divine power which desires to control everything they do and say. This power cannot be seen on an X-ray or image scan because it is invisible. It is like electricity—we can see what it does (the effects,) but we can't see it running through the wire. This power is the Holy Spirit which has been a controversial topic throughout the history of religion.

In the movie "Star Wars," the good guys believed in a mysterious force which guided and protected them in the struggle between good and evil. They parted company with the words, "May the force be with you." Likewise, there is a marvelous force which lives and works in the hearts and lives of God's people. This powerful force, the Holy Spirit, was active in the creation of the world (Genesis 1:2) and can be seen throughout the Bible history of God's people.

What Do We Know About the Holy Spirit?

The inspired Scriptures tell us that the Holy Spirit is the third person in the trinity which is difficult for human beings to comprehend (1 John 5:8). He is a divine personality equal to the Father and the Son who works in unison with the Father and Son. Jesus always referred to the Spirit with the pronouns "he" and "him," not "it." The author will use the same pronouns. The Holy Spirit is omnipotent and omnipresent (Psalms 139:7). He was active in the Old Testament as well as New Testament times. He worked amazing signs and wonders through Jesus and the early disciples (Hebrews 2:4). We know that He lives in the hearts and bodies of Christians today (Romans 8:9; 1 Corinthians 6:19). The Holy Spirit is real; He is not a phantom or figment of our imagination.

How does He get inside of God's children? God places the Holy Spirit in the hearts of believers when they repent and are baptized in the name of Christ (Acts 2:38). It is similar to the way a newborn inherits the genes and chromosomes of its parents. When new Christians are born, God gives them His Spirit as a gift to live in them, to help them grow and mature, and to empower them to be like the Father. The Holy Spirit dwells within all who have a relationship with God.

The Holy Spirit empowered New Testament Christians to perform various tasks necessary to the development of the early church. Even though spiritual gifts varied from one believer to another, there were some functions of the Spirit that were common to all Christians. Many of these functions were explained by the Apostle Paul in his letter to the Romans.

What Does the Holy Spirit Do?

According to Romans, the Holy Spirit help us control the evil desires of the body (Romans 8:13). People who have a relationship with God are not perfect individuals. The old desires of lust, rage, hate, and greed don't die easily. Sometimes, they play dead but come alive again in moments of weakness and temptation. The Spirit within us gives us the courage and power to say "no" to the evil one. When tempted, God will always "give us a way of escape," but sometimes because of our own weakness we choose not to listen to the Holy Spirit within us (1 Corinthians 10:13). Relationship people are not robots; sometimes they get tripped up by sin. God's children however, usually sin less than people without a relationship with

God because the Holy Spirit is at work in our lives and helps us with our weaknesses (Romans 8:26). Another great advantage of a relationship with God is the realization that his constant grace covers our sin (1 John 2:1). The Holy Spirit strives to keep Christians pure and purified. If we persist in a sin and ignore the Spirit's warnings, however, we are in danger of "putting out the Spirit's fire" in our hearts.

The Holy Spirit also helps us to pray more effectively. All people who have a right relationship communicate with God to some degree, but sometimes we lack the wisdom to know how to pray. Sometimes we ask for the wrong things and neglect to pray for the important things. Sometimes we lack the faith to put our complete trust in the God who answers prayer and we get frustrated. Romans says the "Spirit himself intercedes for us with groans that words cannot express" (Romans 8:26). The intercession of the Holy Spirit is an exciting concept to think about. There are therefore two dimensions to prayer—what we contribute and what the Spirit contributes. The Holy Spirit is the Christian's prayer partner. He is praying with us and for us and His contribution is infallible. If we forget to mention a particular sin, He does it for us. If we forget a particular need, the Spirit mentions it for us. If we fall asleep in the middle of a prayer, the Spirit finishes the prayer for us. When we have a relationship with God, we also have a relationship with His Spirit. We have the assurance that the Spirit is our friend and He is always there for us even when we are unaware of His presence.

The Holy Spirit protects us and seals us against the power of Satan. Paul wrote in Ephesians 1:13-14 that the saved were "marked with a seal, the promised Holy Spirit, who is a deposit guaranteeing our inheritance." The concept of a seal had great significance in the first century. The Roman seal was placed on every government document. The Roman seal was placed over the tomb of Jesus. The Roman seal identified the document or property as belonging to Caesar. Breaking that seal without proper authority was punishable by death. Likewise, God's seal (the Holy Spirit in our hearts) protects us from Satan and his demons. The seal of the Spirit means every Christian is "God's property" and it screams out to Satan, "This soul is my property and you can't have him!" God has an investment in each of His children and He will not allow Satan to steal us away.

Another function of the Holy Spirit is to produce Christ-like fruit in our lives. The fruit, listed in Galatians 5:22, are "love, joy, peace, patience, kindness, goodness, faithfulness, gentleness, and self-control." Such fruit are unnatural for human beings. People who have no relationship with God are greedy, self-centered, and worldly. God's people are "other-worldly" in their attitude and actions. Christians yield beautiful fruit that make them attractive to all with whom they come in contact. The fruit of the Spirit have a greater impact on the world than many of the more sensational works of the Spirit from Bible times such as tongues, healings, and eloquence. The fruit of the Spirit enable Christians to be the "salt of the earth" and the "light of the world" in whatever circumstance they find themselves. Spirit people will shine the light of God from prisons, from poverty, and from kings' palaces. Look at the amazing stories of Joseph, Daniel, Esther, and Paul. When Peter and John stood before the Jewish council "the Jewish leaders were astonished at them and took note that these men had been with Jesus" (Acts 4:13).

Don't Put Out the Spirit's Fire

The Holy Spirit is all powerful and He wants control of our lives for good. Some people are control freaks and they struggle with the Spirit for control. They are willing to practice religion as long as they can be in control. That's why it is so important for God's people to strive for total dependence on God. If we have the right relationship with God, we will attempt to yield all control to his Spirit and let go of our own selfish will.

God's people will never understand everything about the Holy Spirit and will never agree on how He works and moves in their lives. The functions discussed in this chapter are not meant to be exhaustive or to limit the workings of the Spirit. Since the Spirit embodies the infinite power of God, then we would have to be God himself to fully comprehend the nature of the Spirit.

Since we don't understand everything about the Spirit, many Christians want to dismiss him completely. Some are quick to deny the Spirit with statements such as, "The Spirit doesn't make people cry or dance for joy today," "He doesn't inspire preachers anymore," "He doesn't speak directly to people's hearts today." "He won't heal people with addictions," "He doesn't heal marriages directly." He doesn't influence churches today." "He doesn't protect people against poison any more." "He doesn't inspire writers or singers today." The Holy Spirit is like a large banquet table that God has prepared for those who love him. Every time we reach for an appealing item on God's table, some well-meaning brother slaps us on the hand and says, "Stop, you can't have that." "Leave that alone, it will just cause trouble." The Spirit can't work in some people today because men won't allow Him to. The Spirit will not work through some Christians because of the hardness of their hearts. No wonder Paul warned, "Do not put out the Spirit's fire" (1 Thessalonians 5:19).

Although 1 Corinthians 13 indicates that some of the Spirit's methods will cease over time, it does not tell us which methods the Spirit might use in the future. The Spirit can work powerfully through the broadcast media, through social media, through medical science, and through computer technology. Although the days of miracle-working men may have passed, the Spirit can still miraculously change individuals, churches, nations, and world events. He will accomplish His work through mortal men and through angels. The unfathomable Spirit can do amazing things in our lives if we will just yield control to Him. There will always be a limit on what the Holy Spirit can do, however, as long as we put Him in a box and define what He can and cannot do in our lives. We should let the Spirit show us what he can do instead of presuming to tell the Spirit what his limits are.

John compared the Spirit to the wind in John 3:8. He said the wind blows wherever it pleases and we hear its sound and see its power, but we cannot understand where it comes from or where it is going. The science of meteorology has come a long way since the first century, but we still shake our heads with amazement when a tornado destroys one house and leaves the next house standing. Likewise, we can see the effects of the Spirit, but we will never understand how He works or what He will do in the future. The Holy Spirit will always be somewhat mysterious to those who have a relationship with God. The Spirit forces us to keep our minds open.

The majority of God's people will agree on certain truths. The Spirit is real; He is here today; He is all-powerful; He is working in our hearts calling us to live holy lives totally dedicated to God. The Spirit protects us from the evil one and assists in our prayer relationship to God. The Spirit enables us to love others, to show kindness to others, and to forgive others even when they nail us to a cross. True forgiveness is the greatest miracle of all.

1. What do we know about the Holy Spirit?
2. How does the Holy Spirit dwell in those who have a relationship with God?
3. Discuss four things the Holy Spirit does to benefit Christians today?
4. How does the Holy Spirit help us in prayer?
5. What does it mean, "Do not put out the Spirit's fire"?
6. Comment on some functions of the Holy Spirit that have ceased and others that have continued?
7. What do you think the author means by putting the Holy Spirit in a box?

8

PRAYER — INSTANT MESSAGING GOD

Every year a man would go duck hunting the day before the season started. The game warden knew about it but had never been able to catch him. One year the warden stationed himself outside the man's house all night in the freezing cold.

At dawn, the hunter yelled out, "Warden, I know you're out there, so come on in."

The warden was flabbergasted and asked the hunter, "How'd you know I was out there?"

The hunter answered, "I didn't, I always shout the same words every year and this was the first time I ever got an answer."

For many Christians, prayer is like that. They have been repeating the same prayers for so long, it would scare them to death if they actually got an answer. Many Christians have been praying all their lives out of duty and tradition. Some pray only in church or when they are in trouble. Prayer is something many people take for granted. They pray the same prayers day after day and get no answers. They get frustrated and feel like giving up but they don't because prayer is something Christians are supposed to do. Prayer, to many Christians, is more of a superstition than a spiritual blessing. They failed to pray once and had an accident, so now they are afraid not to pray. They are prisoners to prayer rather than practitioners of prayer. How do Christians ever know that God answers prayers? If one believes, no proof is necessary; if he does not believe, no proof is sufficient. God requires an attitude of belief in prayer.

In a world of text messaging and instant messaging, we sometimes forget that prayer is a direct channel of communication created by God himself to keep to touch with His children. Adam and Eve talked directly with God but soon afterward, God's servants used prayer to communicate with the Father. Prayer goes to the heart of God anytime of the day or night.

One of the greatest problems affecting Christians today is that they have lost faith in the power of prayer. Prayer is the most powerful force in the universe. According to a famous quotation often attributed to Abraham Lincoln, "Prayer moves the hand that moves the world." We have God's infinite power at our disposal if we just ask according to His will. Deists claim that God set the universe in motion and then withdrew from intervening in people's lives. But that makes God remote and unapproachable. If we believe God is unapproachable then we have no reason to try to communicate with Him.

According to a survey by Princeton University researchers, 87% of Americans believe God answers prayer. Fifty-four percent pray at least once a day and 29% pray more than once a day. Fifty-four percent say that when God doesn't answer their prayers, it means it wasn't God's will and 82% do not turn away from God when prayers go unanswered. Eighty-two percent pray for the health or success of family members, 75% pray for strength to overcome personal weakness, 73% pray for help in finding a job, 79% say God answers prayers for healing someone with an incurable disease, 51% think God doesn't answer prayers to win sporting events, and 36% do not believe in praying for financial or career success.[1]

People who have a relationship with God believe prayer is one of the greatest blessings of the Christian life. It's a privilege and an honor to able to talk to almighty God. Just as a deep sea diver has a line that supplies oxygen from the ship above, Christians have a lifeline that connects them to their Heavenly Father at all times. My mother lives in another state and it is very comforting to know that there is a telephone linking my house to hers. My adult children communicate regularly through e-mail. Today, most people, including grade-school children, carry mobile phones with them at all times. I've read that the average teenager text-messages and checks his or her Facebook account 200 times a day—often while they are sitting in class or driving. The desire to keep in touch is overwhelming. Think of prayer as our instant message to God. He is our Father and wants us to stay in touch with us at all times because we are family and He loves us.

Communication is crucial to any relationship. Lack of communication is one of the top reasons marriages fail. Lack of communication is also one of the top reasons believers fall away from God. To have a relationship we have to tell each other what's going on. God wants us to tell Him what's going on and what concerns us. God has told His people that He is always available and will hear and answer our prayers according to His will (1 John 5:13-14). A person with a relationship with God communicates with God continually. God is the first person he speaks to upon waking in the morning and the last person he speaks to when lying down. A relationship person talks to God throughout the day—before meals, in times of stress, in times of concern, in times of temptation, in times of pain, and in times of decision. We can pour out our hearts to Him, make requests for ourselves or intercede for others, we can express thanksgiving and joy to Him, we can ask forgiveness, we can praise Him and magnify His name.

Prayers God Listens To

God has placed some conditions on answered prayer. He makes it clear in the Old Testament that a person who holds unrepented-of sin in his heart and life will not be heard. "Your iniquities have separated you from your God; your sins have hid his face from you so that he will not hear" (Isaiah 59:2). Some people want to hold on to their sin and still be on speaking terms with God. You can't have it both ways. Many are like the little boy who prayed, "God, if it's your will make me a better boy; but don't worry if you can't, 'cause I'm having a good time the way I am."

God will not hear a person who refuses to listen or heed God's

Word. "If anyone turns a deaf ear to the law, even his prayers are detestable" (Proverbs 28:9). God will listen to any person who has a receptive heart.

God will not answer selfish prayers. James 4:3 warns, "When you ask, you do not receive, because you ask with the wrong motives that you may spend what you get on your pleasures." This is a difficult passage for most Christians. The statistics given earlier mentioned praying for victory in sports or for more success in your job. I believe those would be selfish prayers. I understand gamblers in Las Vegas pray before they throw the dice. Any prayer for more money, a bigger house, a better job when He has already blessed us with plenty would qualify as a selfish prayer. Everyone with a right relationship with God will be very reluctant to ask for selfish requests. The humble preacher, Batsell B. Baxter, told me before cancer took his life that he never asked God for healing for himself because he considered that a selfish prayer. He prayed only for strength for himself and for the welfare of his beloved survivors.

God has told us that he will gladly hear the prayers of the humble. The publican described in Luke 18 cried, "Lord, be merciful to me a sinner" and his prayer was heard. This man was not a Pharisee or a Christian, but God loved him for his beautiful, humble heart. The psalmist wrote, "He will respond to the prayer of the destitute" (Psalms 102:17). A person who is destitute is down and out—no friends, no money, no food, no hope, no place to turn but God.

Prayer is more about our attitude than it is the words we say or the thoughts we express. To pray effectively, we must have an attitude of unworthiness and total dependence on God. This attitude will change our lives even if God does not intervene.

God will answer the prayers of those who ask in faith. James wrote, "If any of you lacks wisdom, let him ask of God who gives generously to all without finding fault, and it will be given to him; but when he asks, he must believe and not doubt, because he that doubts is like a wave of the sea, blown and tossed by the wind. That man should not think he will receive anything from the Lord" (James 1:5-7). It's easy to ask but it's hard to believe you will receive. Jesus explains it clearly in Mark 11:24 when He said, "Whatever you ask for in prayer, believe that you have received it, and it will be yours." Jesus is asking the believer to picture the prayer as answered in his mind while he is praying.

Keys to More Effective Prayer

A study of the prayers of our Lord indicates two kinds of prayer. The first kind we will call spontaneous prayers. These are the quick, spontaneous prayers we say throughout the day. Due to the feelings of the moment or the need of the hour, Jesus often prayed brief prayers as he did when he raised Lazarus or prayed from the cross, "Father forgive them for they know not what they do." Christians with a relationship with God have a constant awareness of God's presence. When we rise in the morning, we say "Thank you for this day." When we're rushed for lunch, we pause momentarily and pray, "Thank you for this food." These are spontaneous, thought prayers. The second kind of prayer is the planned, worship prayer. Effective worship requires a certain amount of time, a quiet setting, and a proper frame of mind. Jesus taught us about worship prayer when He got up before daylight and found a solitary place for extended prayer (Mark 1:35). He prayed all night before choosing

A Relationship With God

His Apostles. Christians need both kinds of prayer. The quick, spontaneous prayers are not sufficient by themselves to handle the weightier burdens of our lives. We need the quiet "sweet hour of prayer" when we can be alone with God and pour our hearts out to Him. The prayers we often neglect are the worship prayers—these are the prayers that lift us up and draw us nearer to God.

1. Make time to pray. Jesus planned times when He could be alone with God. According to one estimate, the average Christian spends just five minutes a day in prayer. We often complain that we don't have the time, but we make time for the newspaper, for television, for the internet, for important business appointments. We often try to fit God into our schedule instead of fitting our schedule around God.

2. Find a quiet place. Jesus suggested going into a closet and shutting the door to be alone. One cannot pray with the kids running through the house or the television blaring. Everyone needs a quiet time—a bedroom, a back yard, a hill top, a walk to be alone with God.

3. Kneel down if possible. We know that kneeling is not commanded, but one's physical posture is important. Many Christians start to pray while lying down only to be frustrated when they fall asleep halfway through. Imagine, having an appointment with the president of the United States and falling asleep in the middle. Kneeling will not only keep us awake, but it is an outward sign of submission and reverence.

4. Pray out loud. This helps to keep our minds on what we're saying. It also makes God seem closer to us—like an intimate friend who is right there with us in the room.

5. Ask God to bless us while we pray. If Satan can't get us to postpone our prayer, he will try to distract us by a ringing phone or a baby's cry. Before we begin, we should ask God to protect us from all distractions. Picture a circle around you and determine that nothing will get through to disturb you as you pray.

6. Remember to confess your sins. Sometimes we have to remind our children, when they come to the table, "Wash you hands first." What if God feels this way? Many Christians begin with all the things they need and forget to confess to God. "If we confess our sins, he is faithful and just and will forgive our sins and purify us from all unrighteousness" (1 John 1:9). Confession and penitence produce a humble attitude which is necessary before God will work in our lives.

7. Pray with thanksgiving. "With thanksgiving present your requests to God." (Philippians 4:6) It's good to take a few minutes to tell God what we're thankful for and avoid using the catch-all phrase, "Thank You for all Your many blessings." We need to name specific blessings, especially those that happened to us the last day or two. I always use my walking time for prayer and when I start listing my blessings, two miles can go by before I realize it.

A Relationship With God

Prayer was part of every great moment in the life of Christ. If God's Son needed strength through prayer in His relationship with God, how much more do God's people today need the power of prayer.

1   Woodland, Kenneth, "Is God Listening," <u>Newsweek</u>, March 31, 1997, pp. 56-65

1. How do Christians know for sure that God has answered prayer?

2. How is text messaging like prayer for people who have a relationship with God?

3. How do your personal beliefs compare with the Princeton University survey?

4. Do you believe God answers prayers to win ball games or to achieve financial success? Where does God draw the line between trivial and serious prayer requests?

5. Does a person have a relationship with God if he fails to communicate? How does the level of communication indicate the level of relationship?

6. What conditions has God placed on acceptable prayer?

7. Explain the two types of prayer in Jesus life. How might these still apply to us today?

8. Share practical ways to make more time for prayer in your life.

9. How important is a "quiet place" in your personal prayer life?

10. Why are confession and thanksgiving important for acceptable prayer?

9

GOD'S WORD — NOURISHMENT FOR THE SOUL

A minister packed his suitcase full except for a tiny space in the corner. "So," he told a friend, "there is still enough room for me to pack a guidebook, a lamp, a mirror, a telescope, a book of poems, a number of biographies, a bundle of old letters, a hymn book, a sharp sword, and a small library of 30 volumes."

His friend asked in amazement, "How can you possibly manage to get all that in the small space you have left?"

"That is easy," said the minister, "for the Bible contains all of these things."

A person who has a relationship with God would not go on a long trip without his Bible. God's Word is as vital to a spiritual relationship as food is to physical life. I have read that every

American military plane that flies over water carries a collapsible boat which contains food rations and a copy of the Bible in a waterproof package. Military officers recognize that spiritual equipment can be as important as food and drink in saving lives.

The Bible Is Forever

After 2,000 years, the Bible is still the world's best-selling book. The French atheist, Voltaire, predicted that the Bible would fall into oblivion, but his own house was later used as a printing place for the Bible. The Apostle Peter states, "You have been born again not of perishable seed but of imperishable, through the living and enduring word of God. . .The grass withers and the flowers fall, but the word of the Lord stands forever" (1 Peter 1:23-24).

The Bible lives forever because it is from God. The Bible contains 66 books written by 40 different men who were kings, fishermen, scholars, prophets, physicians, tax collectors, and farmers who never knew one other. It was written over a period of 1,600 years in different languages and different cultures; yet all the books of the Bible present one central theme. The amazing miracle of the Bible's existence is explained simply by Paul in 2 Timothy 3:16 as "divine inspiration."

The Bible lives forever because it deals with eternal truths. The Bible is never out of date for it tells where man is from, where he is going, why he is here, and how he should live while he is here on earth. It deals with the greatest principles of ethics: love, justice, righteousness, truth, beauty, and self-disciplined obedience to God.

The Bible lives forever because it meets man's needs. Human

nature has not changed. People still have the same longings, the same need for guidance, and the same need for redemption that they always have had. Honesty, integrity, truth, virtue, self-control, brotherly-love, goodness, and purity are as important in the 21st century as they were in the first.

We have no new problems, or needs, or temptations, or sins. Our great bewildering task in this rapidly changing world is to distinguish between those things which are lasting and eternal and those things which are temporary and fleeting. The Word of God is our eternal guide by which to measure and evaluate all things.

God's Neglected Love Letter to Man

In spite of the Bible's power and message it is the most neglected book in the world. Most religious people have more than one copy of the Bible in their homes but never take time to read it. The Bible adorns lamp tables and bookshelves, gathering dust while people perish without spiritual direction. Perhaps you have heard the story about the old man who discovered several thousand dollars in a family Bible. Forty years previous his aunt had died and her will read, "To my beloved nephew Steven, I will and bequeath my family Bible and all it contains, with the residue of my estate after my funeral expenses and just and lawful debts are paid." The estate amounted to a few hundred dollars which were soon spent and for forty years the man had lived in poverty. All that time, within his reach, there was the precious Bible containing thousands of dollars, sufficient for all his wants. What regrets must have filled his mind. If he only had opened that Bible years ago, he might have used the money to great advantage. This is a sad story but not nearly as sad as the neglect of the Bible by religious people. In God's book the riches of His wisdom and grace are made known. We cannot force people to open the book and read the Word of God. Only by sharing about one's relationship with God can a person influence others to investigate the riches of God's Word for themselves.

A love letter is very special to a person who is in love. The Bible has been called God's love letter to mankind. God gave us the Bible because He is in love with us and wants to redeem us as His sons and daughters. All who have a relationship with God understand His love and His love letter (which we call the Bible) is very special to us. We love God because He first loved us and we want to communicate with God because He first communicated with us. We love His word and cling to it like a love letter from a beloved friend.

People use the Bible for many purposes. They take oaths on it in trials and weddings, save their family photographs in it, and press flowers and other keepsakes between its pages. But people who have a true relationship with God know and love their Bible. Their Bible is a treasure from God and they study it diligently knowing it is their guidebook to heaven.

How to Study the Bible

People have many different methods of reading the Bible. I believe some of these methods are ineffective and unprofitable for serious growth and development. I will list several methods which are less than satisfying for a serious Bible student. The first is the "open and point" method used by many people for devotional readings. Some feel this method allows the Spirit to guide them much like a ouija board. If one is lucky enough to hit the Proverbs, one might gain a meaningful thought or two, but generally, miscellaneous material taken out of context is meaningless and often confusing.

Another widely-used method which I have found to be of limited value is the yearly calendar with daily scheduled readings. There are 1,189 chapters in the Bible so most daily reading schedules cover three or more chapters a day which is a heavy burden for most people. The reading assignments are so heavy that readers have no opportunity to study the purpose, background, and commentary on the chapters assigned. My experience has been that I always get behind and then have to read twelve chapters to get back on schedule. This only compounds the problem. People who follow this method often read the Bible out of a sense of duty, "doing their task for the day," rather than reading out of a desire for enlightenment.

The only Bible study many Christians get is in a scheduled church Bible class or small group discussion. A well-structured class taught by a well-prepared, skilled teacher has many advantages over the previous methods. One common problem found in many Bible classes is the tendency to hear twenty peoples' opinions about what a verse means instead of a first-hand study of what the inspired author meant in the verse. Since many of these opinions are out in left field and often contradictory, one leaves the class just as puzzled as he was when he came in.

If the only Bible study one gets is a twenty minute sermon or two every Sunday, a person will suffer from spiritual anorexia. Sermons are inspirational, practical, and sometimes entertaining but sermons are not intended to offer in-depth Bible instruction. Many have aided their listening by developing the habit of taking notes. Others like to underline passages and write notes in their Bibles. Christians in the first century, lacking any Christian writings, had no choice but to rely on the spoken word as the source of their knowledge. When an apostle came to town, he would teach daily in the synagogues, public gathering places, and people's homes. Serious disciples would sit day after day, for hours at a time, soaking up every word. Today's equivalent to the first century experience would include lectureships, seminars, workshops, and institutes for intensified Bible study.

Serious Bible readers should always begin their study with prayer. We should ask God to give us insights as we read that will bless our lives. We should always study with an open mind to let God speak to us through His Word rather than reading to confirm preconceived notions we already have about a book or passage. We need to let God tell us what He wants us to know rather than telling Him what He is allowed to say. An open mind is precious in the eyes of God and often He will bless us with new thoughts that will "knock our socks off."

I believe there are two methods of Bible study that are particularly worthwhile in fostering a relationship with God. One is an in-depth topical study. Every home should have a topical Bible or a detailed concordance, which allows a person to study every Bible reference on a particular topic such as prayer or sacrifice. An internet search engine can also be helpful in a topical study. One problem is that some words in the Bible have more than one meaning. The word "cry," for example, doesn't always mean expressing sorrow. "Cried to the Lord," frequently refers to prayer. Words such as "cup" and "adultery" have several meanings determined only by the context.

The most valuable method of Bible study is the detailed textual study. A textual study takes a Bible text in its entirety and begins with the historical background, the geography, the writer, the purpose, and the theme. Then the study proceeds verse by verse with scholarly commentary including explanations of significant Hebrew or Greek words which shed light on the text. There are books containing textual studies on any part of the Bible. If you live in an area where a Christian university or Bible college is located, I would strongly recommend auditing or taking a Bible course on campus. Many state universities also have Bible chairs with religious courses taught by qualified instructors. Some colleges and preacher training schools have Bible courses available through workbooks, correspondence courses, CD's and DVD's. The Internet has a whole world of distance learning opportunities for serious Bible students. Most Christian colleges and universities offer electronic Bible courses. One can find out which courses are available by looking at the websites of Christian schools which are advertised in religious publications. The Internet also offers numerous opportunities for Bible study with more than a million possible sites on the word "Bible" alone.

I believe it is beneficial to group the Bible books together in units and not to pick books at random. It's helpful to study Genesis to Esther together because these books give the history of God's ancient people. Job through Song of Solomon are poetry and must be read as such. Isaiah to Malachi contain the words of the prophets.

Matthew through Acts are crucial to every Christian because they tell us about Jesus and our goal is to become more like him. Romans through Revelation are letters which contain Christian doctrine.

Martin Luther said he studied his Bible as he gathered apples. First, he shook the whole tree, that the ripest might fall; then he shook each limb, and when he had shaken each limb, he shook each branch, and after each branch, every twig; and then he looked under every leaf. His advice is still valid today. We should search the Bible as a whole, shaking the whole tree. Then shake every limb—study book after book. Then shake every branch, giving attention to each chapter until a complete thought is finished. Then shake each twig, by a careful study of the paragraphs and sentences. Finally, look under each leaf by searching the meaning of the words.

Those who have a relationship with God will have a hunger for God's Word that will last a lifetime. Only with serious study will our relationship grow and mature.

1. Why does the military include a Bible in their survival equipment?

2. What is today's best-selling book? Why do people continue to purchase so many Bibles?

3. What is today's most neglected book? Why?

4. Why has the Bible been called God's love letter to mankind?

5. How effective is one sermon a week for our spiritual nutrition?

6. Describe two worthwhile methods of Bible study.

7. Why is it beneficial to study the Bible books in groups such as history, poetry?

8. What does apathy toward the Bible say about a person's relationship with God?

10

A RELATIONSHIP BRINGS GOD'S GIFTS

The story is told about a homeless man in New York City who dressed in rags and begged for food for 30 years. One day he begged money from a well-dressed man who turned out to be his long-lost brother.

"Charlie, is that you?" his brother asked. "We've been looking everywhere for you. Dad died almost 30 years ago and left you a fortune. You had already left home and we could not locate you to tell you about it."

This "rags to riches" story is both tragic and joyful. Charlie had lived in misery for 30 years, when all that time he was rich and didn't know it. Those are 30 years he can never get back. Just think what he could have accomplished in life if he had not had to beg for his daily existence.

The man in this story was rich because of his relationship to his earthly father.

He was not rich because of anything he had done in his life. He was not even aware of his inheritance until his brother told him. Many people today do not realize what rich gifts are available from God because no one has informed them.

All who have a relationship with God are extremely rich, although many go through life without realizing it. Paul reminds the Ephesians, "Praise be to the God and Father of our Lord Jesus Christ….who has blessed us with every spiritual blessing in Christ" (Ephesians 1:3). Verse seven says, "God has lavished on us the riches of his grace." The word "rich" is used six times in Ephesians. Jesus died and left us a fortune. God has no children who are not rich. If we realized how rich we are we would be more enthusiastic in our Christian service.

Having a personal relationship with God is like being a child on Christmas morning. Except that God's gifts are far more exciting than toys or socks. Imagine what it must have been like for the Israelites in the wilderness who woke up every morning to see the ground covered with manna, white flakes of bread, from heaven. God also gave them a pillar of cloud by day and a pillar of fire by night, visible reminders of his care and protection. They received gifts of quail from heaven and water which flowed from rocks. God gave them the law, the tabernacle, miraculous victories in battle, as well as the ultimate earthly gift—the Promised Land. Yet the people murmured and complained the whole way. They certainly did not feel rich even though they had God's visible presence and wagon loads of gold and Egyptian treasure. Of course God's spiritual gifts, His love and care, were worth infinitely more than the gold and treasure. The gold just got them in trouble. God continues to shower us with physical and spiritual gifts every day. Like the Israelites however, we often forget the source and take God's gifts for granted.

Consider the Source

James writes, "Every good and perfect gift is from above, coming down from the Father" (James 1:17). God enjoys giving gifts to His children. The best-known verse in the New Testament begins with the words, "God so loved the world that he *gave* His one and only son" (John 3:16). God is the world's greatest giver. He expects us to be grateful recipients of His grace. God not only gave His Son, but He keeps on giving to those with whom He has a relationship. In the chapters of this book you have read about the gift of the Holy Spirit which God gives to every believer. You have read about the gifts of the Spirit, "love, joy, peace, patience, kindness, goodness, faithfulness, gentleness, self-control," which bloom in every Christian's life. You have read about the gift of salvation which does not come through our works but God's grace. You will also read about the gift of eternal life that God gives to all who have a relationship with Him.

Once a tax auditor came to a poor servant of God to determine the amount of taxes he would have to pay. "How would you describe your property?" asked the auditor.

"Oh, I am very wealthy," replied the Christian.

"List your possessions please." The auditor instructed.

"First, I have everlasting life (John 3:16). Second, I have a mansion in heaven (John 14:2 KJV). Third, I have peace that transcends understanding (Philippians 4:7). Fourth, I have inexpressible joy (1 Peter 1:8). Fifth, I have divine love that never fails (1 Corinthians 13:8). Sixth, I have a faithful wife (Proverbs 31:10). Seventh, I have obedient children (Exodus 20:12). Eighth, I have loyal friends (Proverbs 18:24). Ninth, I have a crown of life (James 1:12). Tenth, I have a savior, Jesus Christ, who supplies all my needs" (Philippians 4:19).

The tax auditor closed his book and said, "Truly you are a rich man, but your property is not subject to taxation."

Many of us are like the tax auditor in the story. When we hear the word "wealth," we think of dollar signs. We think of winning the lottery and having money in the bank. The riches that come from a relationship with God are primarily spiritual in nature. Money cannot buy peace of mind, or the forgiveness of sins, or a pure conscience, or a home in heaven. Only a relationship with God can supply our deepest needs. In this life, we often get our needs and our wants mixed up. We want things we don't need and sometimes we need things we don't want. We want that big piece of cheesecake, but we might need to go on a diet. It sounds so simple but it's not. I treasure my relationship with my grandchildren. I recently tried to explain to my three-year old grandson why he should not do something. He replied, "But I really, really want to." At least he was honest about it.

God is not in the business of giving new cars, vacations, or lottery jackpots. This is not to say that God will not answer our prayers for the remission of cancer or for a job so that we can support our families. Some servants of God, however, suffer inexplicably and live short lives. Some die with their children in tragic accidents and some die martyrs to their faith. But they receive the same spiritual blessings as the rest of us—perhaps more. Paul was given an extra measure of grace to help him bear the thorn in the flesh that caused him pain (2 Corinthians 12:9).

Certain television evangelists promise that God will give health, wealth, and prosperity to all who dig deep and send a generous gift to their ministry. This *"quid pro quo,"* "tit for tat" Christianity" deceives a lot of people, but it is not biblical. Jesus promised that if we are called to sacrifice for His name's sake "we will receive a hundred times as much and will inherit eternal life" (Matthew 19:29). Jesus is saying that spiritual blessings are worth a hundred times as much as the things we have to sacrifice for Him. God teaches us to be gracious givers, but not for the purpose of getting back rewards.

God's Gifts Are Forever

God knows what we need because he has a relationship with us and he gives us spiritual gifts throughout our lives. These gifts are secure because they are "in Christ." These two significant words are found 14 times in Ephesians 1 and used 150 times in the New Testament. Everyone who has a relationship with the Father is "in Christ" and everyone who is "in Christ" enjoys this special relationship. Christ and His Father are one.

Many people today are obsessed with home security. They invest in safes, alarms, and sophisticated anti-theft devices to protect their jewelry and valuables. Ecclesiastes tells about the folly of the rich man who cannot sleep at night from worrying about his possessions. We can lose our physical possessions in a flash. All it takes is an earthquake, a tornado, a fire, or a thief. That's why Jesus urged us to store up our "treasures in heaven where moth and rust do not destroy and where thieves do not break in and steal" (Matthew 6:20). God's gifts are treasures we will keep for eternity.

Some Christians worry about losing the gift of eternal life. Our eternal reward is safe because its safety does not depend on a place or on our own feeble efforts. God's gift of eternal life is safe "in Christ."

Let's praise God for His wonderful gifts. Nothing love can give has been withheld from us. He has given everything we need to be happy, to grow spiritually, go bear fruit, to be strong in Christ, and to go to heaven.

While it's true that all spiritual gifts come from our relationship with God, the very privilege of divine relationship itself is a precious gift. Aren't you glad our God is not a distant God who has no desire to have a relationship with His creation? Some may wish to ignore God and pretend He is far away or nonexistent, but He does not wish to ignore us and that is good news.

1. What does it mean to say that "children of God are rich"?
2. Why weren't the Israelites more grateful after all the gifts God gave them?
3. God's gifts today are primarily spiritual gifts. Agree or disagree?
4. What's wrong with "prosperity evangelism"?
5. Why are God's gifts to us secure "in Christ?"
6. What might interfere with God's gift of eternal life?
7. What did Jesus mean when He said to "store up our treasures in heaven?"

11

SHIPWRECKED — A BROKEN RELATIONSHIP

A broken relationship is the most painful thing on earth. That's why divorce and job loss are so devastating. Our society has tried to devise a painless divorce called "no fault" divorce, but it is really a misnomer. No divorce is painless and there is usually fault on both sides.

In a broken relationship with God there is no such thing as a "no fault" separation because God is faultless and man is always at fault.

Once a man complained to a minister that his relationship with God had deteriorated, "I just don't feel close to God anymore."

The minister replied, "God hasn't moved."

If God hasn't moved, it's obvious who has moved. Isaiah 59

paints a sad picture. "Surely the arm of the Lord is not too short to save nor his ear too dull to hear, but your iniquities have separated you from your God. Your sins have hidden his face from you so that he will not hear" (Isaiah 59:1-2).

Shipwrecked Faith

What a hopeless and desolate condition to be separated from God. For a person who once had a relationship with God to lose that relationship is indeed life's greatest tragedy. In his first letter to Timothy, Paul warned, "Hold on to faith and a good conscience. Some have rejected these and so have shipwrecked their faith. Among them are Hymenaeus and Alexander, whom I have handed over to Satan to be taught not to blaspheme" (1 Timothy 1:19, 20). Long before automobile wrecks, train wrecks, bombs, and airplane crashes, the greatest tragedy known to the ancient world was a shipwreck. A shipwreck was nearly always fatal to everyone on board. The Titanic was the largest passenger ship in the world in 1912 when she sank resulting in 1,517 deaths.

Paul uses a shipwreck to explain the tragedy of separation from God. Paul knew what it meant to suffer shipwreck having twice survived such a tragedy (2 Corinthians 11:25). He mentions two men who had shipwrecked their faith. At one time, these men had a relationship with God and were traveling toward the port of heaven. But something terrible happened.

A broken relationship implies that it is possible to fall from grace. Although some churches promote the doctrine of "once in grace, always in grace," Paul's warning to the Galatians, "you have fallen away from grace," would seem to put that doctrine to rest

(Galatians 5:4). I believe it is a matter of semantics. God's grace is certainly sufficient to forgive us, save us, and keep us in a saved relationship as long as we cooperate, but His grace will not force a person to stay in the relationship against his will. In that case, grace would no longer be a free gift; it would be coercion. It would be better to rephrase the doctrine, "once in grace, always in grace as long as I want to be in grace." It is not God's will to lose any of his children, but it happens. A coach does not want to lose any games, but it happens. A newlywed never intends for his marriage to break up, but it happens.

No Christian ever has to experience shipwreck. The Holy Spirit protects us and helps us control the desires of the flesh. God has promised that He will never allow us to be tempted above what we are able to bear and will always provide a way of escape (1 Corinthians 10:13). God will do His part if we will do our part. When Paul was on the ship bound for Rome in Acts 27, he tried to warn the centurion about the danger ahead. If the captain had listened to Paul, the ship would not have wrecked. As we travel toward heaven, there are certain warning signs that will help us avoid a shipwreck of our relationship with God. There is one difference between a literal shipwreck and a spiritual shipwreck: in a real shipwreck a passenger has no control. In a spiritual shipwreck a Christian has the control in his hands and can avoid tragedy by heeding the warning signs.

Warning Signs

One warning sign of shipwreck is forsaking your first love. Christ gives this warning to the church at Ephesus in

Revelation 2:4. A lot of marriages fail because the partners fall out of love. Sometimes they find a new love that replaces the first love. The Christians at Ephesus had stopped loving God. They were once strong and active but had stopped growing, praying, studying, worshiping, and depending on God. They had neglected the Christian disciplines, those little acts of love that keep the flame of love burning brightly in one's heart. The symptoms of spiritual decline are similar to the decline of physical health. It generally begins with a loss of appetite for wholesome food—prayer, Bible study, and devotional reading. When you perceive these symptoms, it's time to be alarmed. You should go immediately to the Great Physician for a cure. A Christian's love for God should grow throughout his lifetime as his relationship with God deepens; it should not diminish. Diminished love is a sign that something is wrong.

Another warning sign of shipwreck is violating your conscience without pain. That is why Paul admonished Timothy, his son in the faith, to "hold on to a good conscience" (1 Timothy 1:19). Your conscience plays an important role in your relationship with God. Conscience is like a compass. If we have received sound training, it will always point in the right direction. It will tell us when we are off course. Violating your conscience will produce guilt, an uncomfortable feeling of pain. A married person does not want to violate his conscience and the first sign of a doomed marriage is when the conscience becomes hardened and calloused. A Christian's conscience is a precious thing in God's sight. He has advised us to follow our conscience in all things. When we feel the pain of guilt, it is time to back away and reexamine our relationship with God.

A Relationship With God

When we cause ourselves pain we also cause God pain.

A third warning sign of spiritual shipwreck is getting caught up in deliberate sin. Hebrews 10:26 warns, "If we deliberately keep on sinning after we have received the knowledge of the truth, no sacrifice for sins is left but only a fearful expectation of judgment." Deliberate sin occurs after the conscience has been ignored. Deliberate sin occurs when a person knows a thing is wrong, has been warned by his own conscience and those who love him, and yet persists in that sin even though he knows it is destroying his relationship with God. Deliberate sin is a sin we are determined to do in spite of all the consequences. Once a person is caught up in deliberate sin, he turns against God and actually blasphemes like the two men Paul mentioned who shipwrecked their faith. A sinner can become so hardened and cynical that he "thumbs his nose" at God.

A final warning sign of spiritual shipwreck is when a Christian practices religion without any relationship (which is the central theme of this book). Jesus called this condition "lukewarm—neither cold nor hot" (Revelation 3:16). We often call it "apathy." A lukewarm Christian may still attend church but has lost his enthusiasm and his joy. He goes through the motions but it doesn't mean anything. Religion for him has become an empty ritual, a meaningless routine to be endured rather than cherished. It would be better for a person to have no religion at all than to have religion without a true relationship with God.

The gravest warnings against breaking relationship with God come not from Paul, but Peter. Peter describes the condition in vivid language, "If they have escaped the corruption of the world by knowing our Lord and Savior Jesus Christ and are again entangled in it and overcome, they are worse off at the end than they were at the beginning. It would have been better for them not to have known the way of righteousness than to have known it and then to turn their backs on the sacred command that was passed on to them. Of them the proverbs are true: A dog returns to its vomit and a sow that is washed goes back to her wallowing in the mud" (2 Peter 2:20-22).

A broken relationship doesn't happen all at once. The last step is only the last of a series of steps before a child of God reaches the verge of the precipice. I believe, further, that even when the edge of the precipice is reached, very few actually jump over. Most people slide down, slowly at first, and it is so easy, so effortless. Only when the pace begins to accelerate terribly, only when control is slipping away, does the pleasant numbness give way to anxiety and alarm. Most shipwrecked Christians never meant to start down the pathway to tragedy. Thankfully, there still exists in most of us a relentless love for the Father and a conscience that never stops working to bring us to our senses.

The greatest tragedy in life is a broken relationship with God. God sent His Son to die on the cross to make a relationship with sinful man possible. When man deliberately breaks off that precious relationship, he is telling God that he doesn't love him anymore and telling Christ that His sacrifice was in vain. Although it breaks God's heart, He never stops loving us. Remember, God is not the one who has moved.

1. How can you compare a shipwreck to a broken relationship with God?
2. Is it possible for a person who is maintaining an intimate relationship with God to "fall from grace"?
3. Can a person fall from grace and still be a religious person? Explain.
4. Discuss the four warning signs mentioned in this chapter.
5. Why is a broken relationship life's greatest tragedy?
6. Explain how guilt can be a positive factor in a Christian's life?
7. How does God respond when we break His heart?

A PERSONAL RELATIONSHIP BRINGS PEACE

On December 24, 1914, trench warfare had become miserable for both armies. It was Christmas Eve and the men on both sides were thinking of home and family. This was not where they wanted to be. From the German side came the song "Silent Night." The British, recognizing the tune, began to sing it in English. Other songs followed.

By day, signs appeared saying "Merry Christmas." Then a soldier from one side invited those from the other to come over and celebrate with them. They met in the middle. By the middle of the day, all along the lines, British and German soldiers were greeting each other in "no man's land." They exchanged food, looked at pictures, and celebrated the day together. The officers were shocked at this and had to literally drive their men back to the trenches for four more years of death and destruction. Clearly, the soldiers longed for peace. It was the political leaders who perpetuated the war.

In the above story, the Prince of Peace overcame war for a moment. He alone can bring peace to this world. He can bring peace to troubled families and churches. He can put peace in a believer's heart that will last forever.

Peace in the Storm

Jesus boarded a small boat with his apostles and pushed out from shore into the Sea of Galilee. The gentle rhythm of the waves was peaceful and soon the Lord was fast asleep. He was still asleep when the storm came. Waves broke over the bow and the boat was nearly swamped. The apostles were terrified and cried out, "Jesus, don't you care if we drown?"

Jesus awakened and asked, "Why are you afraid? Where is your faith?" Then he turned toward the water and uttered three simple words, "Peace, be still." The wind immediately died down and the sea became as glass once again. The men were amazed and asked, "What kind of man is this? Even the winds and the waves obey him" (Matthew 8:23-27).

The apostles learned an important lesson that day. People who have a right relationship with God always experience peace even in the midst of life's storms. Our world has seen some devastating wars and violent disasters. Our nation has been racked by the attack on the World Trade Center, bombings, and mass shootings. Every day we read of crime, killing, and violence in schools and work places. We search for peace in our homes, but often they are scenes of fighting and domestic violence. The only place were we would expect to always find peace, the church, often let's us down. We hear peace, love, and unity preached from the pulpits, but sometimes we find division and strife in the membership.

We all desire peace in our personal lives, but we find storms everywhere we turn—sickness, sorrow, pain, disappointments, setbacks, and death. We crave peace in this world, but we cannot find it. Some use pills, needles, and alcohol to ease their pain. But real peace is not found in life, in things, or in the world. Real peace is found in a person.

The Prince of Peace

Jesus was called the "Prince of Peace." When he was born, the angels sang, "Glory to God in the highest and on earth peace to those on whom God's favor rests" (Luke 2:14). Most people have taken this passage to mean the end to wars, peace between nations of the world. But this wasn't the peace Jesus came to bring. When Jesus was born, the world was at peace. The Roman Empire declared in 29 B.C. that peace would be maintained throughout the empire—"pax romana." Jesus himself predicted that there would be wars and rumors of wars until the end of time. The worst wars that have ever been fought have taken place after His visit to the earth. What the angels in Luke 2 actually promised was personal peace to all those who have a relationship with God. Jesus came to bring inner peace for the human soul. Jesus explained the peace He would give in His farewell message to His disciples (John 14:27). He said, "Peace I leave with you, my peace I give you. I do not give to you as the world gives. Do not let your hearts be troubled and do not be afraid."

The source of Jesus' peace was the relationship He had with His father. The peace He received from heaven kept Him serene in the face of danger, calm under the worst circumstances. Jesus wanted His disciples to have the same calm disposition He did. Remember, He was giving this inner peace to quick-tempered Peter, to James and John (Sons of Thunder), and to Simon the Zealot, a former member of a politically violent group.

Jesus' peace was not what the world gives. The world gives the peace of money, security, and good health. Jesus' peace comes from the heart and the conscience. It is the antidote to all of life's troubles and it is superior to all outward circumstances. Think of all the millions of Christians who suffered martyrdom for Christ. The world tried its best to take peace away from Christians, but it did not succeed. Many Christians died singing hymns to God as they fell in the sand of the Roman Colosseum. Persecution cannot take away our peace. The world can put us in prison, steal our money, take our jobs away, kill our loved ones, and take our lives, but no can ever take away our peace.

When Jesus appeared to His disciples after His resurrection, He said, "Peace be with you" (John 20:19). Nineteen of the 27 epistles in the New Testament begin with the greeting, "Grace and Peace to you . . . ." For years, I wondered why the words grace and peace always occurred together. Later, I came to the realization that without grace there is no peace. Without the knowledge that Jesus died to take away our sins and that God's mercy is "new every morning," we cannot rest mentally because of the guilt and worry of never knowing for sure if we're saved. Only with the security of salvation found in God's grace, comes the peace of mind that gives confidence and hope to every Christian.

What was it that enabled first century Christians to walk into the Roman Colosseum to their death singing praises to God? They demonstrated incredible strength under intolerable, deadly conditions. They surely had the "peace that transcends all understanding that will guard your hearts and minds in Christ Jesus," that Paul spoke about in Philippians 4:7. The secret of their strength was their relationship with the living God. Everyone who has a personal relationship with God has the spirit of peace in his heart which no one can take away.

Freedom from Worry

In the well-known words of Psalms 23, "The Lord is my shepherd, I shall not want." The sheep had nothing to worry about when the shepherd was on duty. His rod, staff, and watchfulness gave them a sense of peace. Christians have nothing to worry about as long as God is in control. He has promised, "I will never leave you or forsake you" (Hebrews 13:5). Some Christians live with constant fear because of a works-based view of salvation. If we are saved according to our works, we can never rest because we never know when we have worked enough. In fact, it is impossible for any Christian to ever work enough to repay God for His overwhelming sacrifice. No Christian can ever work enough to merit his salvation. My heart goes out to the generations of Christians who grew up in earlier centuries in an oppressive climate of worry and fear. A person who believes he can get to heaven by works is like a world-class high jumper attempting to jump a chasm 100 yards wide. Even if he can jump 10 yards, he will still fall short because the distance is humanly impossible. We all need the grace of God to make up for our inadequacies. God's grace removes all the worry and gives us peace that comforts our hearts through life and even in death.

I heard about a farm hand who applied for a job. In his interview with the farm owner, he was asked to describe his strongest asset. He replied, "I can sleep when the storms come." The farm hand was saying that he believed in preparing so thoroughly that he could rest with confidence that the animals and buildings were all locked up safely. The farm hand got the job. Once a person has accepted the lordship of Christ and has a personal relationship with God, the peace of God fills his heart and he, like the farm hand, can rest when the storms come.

The beautiful Hebrew word for peace, "shalom," is recognized around the world. Shalom actually means more than just peace or a greeting. It includes completeness, wholeness, and perfect safety. Only God has the power to make us complete and perfectly safe. The Psalmist wrote, "I will lie down and sleep in peace for you alone, O Lord, make me dwell in safety" (Psalms 4:8).

God's Peace Is Eternal

Since our relationship with God is eternal, the peace that God gives will fortify Christians through all the trials of life and continue to comfort them across the river of death. In John's vision of God in Revelation 4, he saw a throne in heaven surrounded by 24 elders dressed in white and 7 lamps symbolizing the Spirit of God. Out of the throne came flashes of lightening and peals of thunder.

Before the throne was a sea of glass, clear as crystal (Revelation 4:6). I believe the sea of glass represents the peace of God that surrounds His throne. God's power may be as awesome as lightening and thunder but His peace is like a calm sea of glass. Lightening and thunder causes turbulence but does not affect the peace which passes understanding. This peace lies deep in the heart of every child of God.

God promised in Ezekiel 37:26, "I will make a covenant of peace with them; it will be an everlasting covenant. I will establish them and increase their numbers, and I will put my sanctuary among them forever."

God's peace sends joy into the heart of every Christian who has a relationship with God. This joy is expressed in the words of the hymn written in 1887 by Peter P. Bilhorn.

> There comes to my heart one sweet strain
> A glad and a joyous refrain
> I sing it again and again,
> Sweet peace, the gift of God's love.

1. What effect does the Prince of Peace have on war on the earth?

2. What kind of peace does a person with a relationship with God have?

3. What was the source of Jesus' peace?

4. Why do the words "grace and peace" so often occur together in the epistles?

5. Why does a "works salvation theology" give no personal peace?

6. What does the "sea of glass" symbolize surrounding God's throne?

7. Why does the peace from God "transcend all understanding?

8. What is the meaning of the Hebrew word "shalom"?

13

A RELATIONSHIP WITH GOD INFLUENCES OTHERS

Tim Tebow has become a household name in America. The former University of Florida quarterback is best-known, however, not for his two national championships or his success as a rookie leading the Denver Broncos to the playoffs. He is known primarily for dropping to one knee after every touchdown in a prayer of thanksgiving to God. His explanation is that he is praising Jesus Christ for giving him the ability and opportunity to be successful. His posture on the field is widely referred to as "Tebowing" and has been copied by youngsters across the country.

Tebow has become the subject of vigorous debate in the media. It seems people would rather talk about him than politics, taxes, or the economy. Many football players, coaches, and sports commentators have criticized him for making a public show of his faith. They feel that religion and football do not mix. Some religious people have criticized him for making a mockery of prayer and being "over the top." After all, Jesus did say in the Sermon on the Mount that we should pray in private. But the Lord also said, in the same sermon, that we should let our light shine and most Christians appreciate Tebow for having the courage to shine his light to millions in the professional football arena.

Whether you appreciate his on-field display or not, you must respect his relationship with God. We are living in a time when schools and businesses feel compelled to call a Christmas tree a "holiday tree" because they are afraid to speak the name of Christ. Too many professional football players have made headlines for drugs, drunkenness, and violence. It's refreshing to see a player who is a visible influence for Christ.

How can a person have a personal relationship with God and not want to share it with his loved ones? How can we keep from telling everyone around us the good news that God wants to have a relationship with them too?

Every person in the Bible who had a relationship with God talked to others about what God had done or was going to do. Most of these people were not called to be prophets or evangelists. They were ordinary people living lives of service to God. Joseph shared his faith in prison and in Pharaoh's palace. Moses also revealed that he had a personal relationship with God. David's relationship with God is evident in every Psalm he wrote.

The New Testament is filled with examples of ordinary people who shared the message of God with others. The mother of Jesus was a shy, teenaged girl, but she testified to her family about what God was doing in her life. The Samaritan woman at the well told a whole city about Christ. Cornelius, the Roman centurion, was very open about his faith. Everyone knew about his generosity and his regular prayer schedule. Tabitha (Dorcas), a poor widow, was well-known for her good works in Joppa. A large crowd of mourners had gathered to honor her influence. Zacchaeus, the chief tax collector in Jericho, invited Jesus into his house. I'm sure this remarkable meeting was the talk of the town. Jesus was moved to say, "Today salvation has come to this house, because this man, too, is a son of Abraham. For the Son of Man came to seek and to save what was lost" (Luke 19:9-10). Zacchaeus was an ordinary man, but he was not afraid to use his influence as a prominent official in Jericho to make a statement about Christ.

This chapter is not intended to produce a burden of guilt on those who have a personal relationship with God. You don't have to join a personal evangelism committee or a door-knocking campaign to please God. Sharing your faith can be summed up as having a positive influence on others. Some people have the gift of talking with people about their faith. Others have the gift of being helpful and doing kind deeds. Still others, have the gift of being good neighbors, good co-workers, good school teachers, good businessmen and women. All of these roles have influence on others.

In the Old Testament, Israel was expected to be a lighthouse to the nations around them. In Isaiah, God said, "I will make you a light for the Gentiles, that you may bring my salvation to the ends of the earth" (Isaiah 49:6). They failed in that mission and became exclusionary and self-centered just as some Christians are today. They believed other nations were not worthy of God's grace and kept Him all to themselves. God finally sent His Son to earth to remind Israel that their mission was to influence all nations.

The Disciples' Commission

Forty days after His resurrection from the dead, Jesus assembled the disciples on the Mount of Olives and told them, "You will be my witnesses in Jerusalem, and in all Judea and Samaria, and to the ends of the earth. After He said this, He was taken up before their very eyes and a cloud hid Him from their sight" (Acts 1:8).

On that same occasion, Jesus commissioned the disciples, "Go and make disciples of all nations, baptizing them in the name of the Father and of the Son and of the Holy Spirit, and teaching them to obey everything I have commanded you. And surely, I am with you always, to the very end of the age" (Matthew 28:19-20). The Greek verb "go" in this passage is a participle which could be translated "while going." We all know missionaries who have devoted a lifetime to foreign evangelism and we respect their sacrifice, but we are not all called to go to distant lands or foreign countries to be missionaries for God. We can be missionaries "while going" to work, going to the store, or going about our chores. We are "on the go" every day and God wants us to be an influence for Him everywhere we go.

Reaching out to people is rooted in the very nature of God. "For God so loved the world that he gave his one and only Son, that whoever believes in him shall not perish but have everlasting life" (John 3:16). God loves all people and wants to draw them into a relationship with Him. God is pictured in the Scriptures as a shepherd seeking lost sheep, as a father seeking a lost son, and as a woman seeking a lost coin. God's love is relentless—He never stops loving and He never stops searching. Neither should we.

Many Christians today have lost all awareness of influencing others for God. We live in a society where a person's religion is a private matter not to be mentioned in public. Modern culture has eroded away our sense of community. We no longer feel a responsibility to reach out to people's hearts and souls. The religious world has substituted a social message in place of the Lord's message. We feel comfortable speaking out against poverty, prejudice, taxes and poor medical care. But we are not sure any longer what our message about God should be.

A Message of What?

In Acts 4, Peter and John were brought before the Jewish council and, "When they saw the courage of Peter and John and realized that they were unschooled, ordinary men, they were astonished and they took note that these men had been with Jesus" (Acts 4:13). Our message today is essentially the same as Peter and John. It's not what we say as much as what people see. Sometimes our nonverbal message is more powerful than our verbal message. People who observe our daily lives should see that we have a relationship with God.

Our message must be based on the assurance that through Christ we have eternal life. We must have the absolute conviction that our salvation is sure. Our salvation must be based on Christ's atonement and the righteousness that comes through him

(2 Corinthians 5:21). If our hope of salvation is based on human effort, we can never be sure of anything. Many Christians attempt to share their faith when they are not sure of their own salvation. A person cannot be an effective spokesman concerning something he doesn't have. Salvation is a gift from God. Only those who realize that gift and the blessed assurance it brings can be a convincing influence on others.

Recently, I heard about two college students who were campaigning door to door in a small town in New England. At one house, a lady with a smile and a kind face answered the door and invited them in for cake and tea. "Tell me again, young man, what you are doing."

"Well, ma'am, we're going through the neighborhood inviting people to a gospel revival, and studying the Bible with anyone who would like to," the young man explained.

"That's wonderful," she replied, "but what is your message?"

"The Bible teaches that we should follow Christ and be saved," they explained.

"I know all that. What has He done for you? What has Jesus done in your life—your every day life? How are you different now that you have Jesus in your life?" she asked.

The young men left her house dazed. They were not able to respond to the most important question of all—Jesus Christ...so what? All other questions are subordinate to this one. We must have an answer. Then we will have our message.

An Influence to Whom?

All around us are people who do not have a relationship with God. They may be friends, co-workers, neighbors, relatives, or strangers. People need our influence and strength the most when they are going through difficult transitions in their lives such as the death of a family member, a divorce, a personal injury, or illness.

We must learn to view people the way Jesus does. In John 9, we read about a man, blind from birth, who had a healing encounter with Christ. Jesus' disciples looked at him as a religious question, "Who sinned, this man or his parents?" His neighbors saw him as a beggar much as we would view a panhandler on the corner today. The Pharisees saw him as a troublemaker and threw him out of the temple. His parents saw him as their blind son. But Jesus looked at this man as an eternal soul. We are all guilty of looking at people from a worldly point of view. Paul, in 2 Corinthians 5:16, wrote, "From now on we regard no one from a worldly point of view. Though we once regarded Christ in this way, we do so no longer." Too often we see a person today as physically attractive, rich, poor, well-educated, young, old, successful, or a member of a particular ethnic group.

When Jesus looked at people, He saw them as eternal souls. He looked at people from a spiritual point of view. When Jesus looked at people, He did not see what they were or what they had been. He saw possibilities in people—what they could become with a relationship with God. The reason this is so important is that we will likely treat people the way we view them. If we see a homeless person as a wino or a loser, we will probably treat them that way.

To be an effective influence on people, we must view them with love and respect. We must befriend people and earn their trust. We need to establish a personal relationship with people before we can be an effective messenger of our relationship with God. We should view people of different faiths as fellow-seekers and friends, not adversaries or prospects. Talking to others about our relationship with God must grow out of a lifestyle that shows "we have been with Jesus."

An effective influence for God must come from genuine joy and enthusiasm. If we aren't excited about our relationship with God, how can we persuade other people to be? Ralph Waldo Emerson once said, "Nothing great is ever accomplished without enthusiasm." The word enthusiasm comes from the Greek word (*enthousiasmos*) which means possessed or inspired by God. Christians are possessed by God and should exude enthusiasm and joy in everything they do. Nothing is more contagious than enthusiasm. It's like wearing a t-shirt with the logo of your favorite sports team. Everyone notices the message and it makes a statement about us. Someone has said, "You cannot kindle a fire in any other heart until it is burning within your own."

1. Name other people in the Bible who had an influence on others?

2. Should only preachers and trained personnel attempt to influence people? Why or why not?

3. Jesus asked his disciples to be His "witnesses." In what ways can we also be witnesses for Christ today?

4. How does the participle "while going" change your view of the Great Commission?

5. What did the council in Jerusalem say about James and John?

6. What is the difference in telling "who" Jesus is and "what he has done in your life?"

7. When do people need our influence the most?

8. How did Jesus view people?

9. What should be our attitude toward people of different faiths?

10. What does enthusiasm have to do with influencing others?

14

A RELATIONSHIP THAT LASTS FOREVER

The best thing about a personal relationship with God is that it never ends. A relationship with God is forever. It sustains us through the hills and valleys of life and carries us through the experience of death. Death is just a door, a passage, through which we pass from one room to another. God promises we will not walk through that door alone. "Even though I walk through the valley of the shadow of death, I will fear no evil, for you are with me; your rod and your staff, they comfort me" (Psalms 23:4). I believe God will send angels to escort us through the door just as He did Lazarus in Luke 16. Death is but an imperceptible moment of time in which a wonderful transition occurs. Heaven's door will open and we will see a glorious banquet of everlasting joys and pleasures reserved for the children of God. Paul said "words cannot express" the glory of God's paradise (2 Corinthians 12:4).

It is not my purpose in this chapter to convince believers that heaven is real because they already know this. But some readers will read the opening paragraph and ask, "What about the final judgment?"

Relationship and the Judgment

The concept of judgment many people have is that of a courtroom where the judge is seated at the bench and lawyers for both sides argue their cases to see which case ultimately wins the judge's (or jury's) decision. The great, final judgment pictured in the New Testament is not an evidentiary trial, but a sentencing hearing. God will not listen to arguments for and against our eternal salvation because He already knows our heart and our life. He already knows who He has pardoned and saved and who He hasn't. He doesn't need for people to plead their case or to stand before Him in suspense waiting for Him to make up His mind. The innocent in our court system are not bound over to sentencing hearings. They do not receive a sentence. Likewise, the righteous are not required to stand in God's judgment. They will receive no sentence.

Many people hold the concept that the judgment is going to be a huge throng of people nervously milling around waiting for their name to be called out on a loud speaker. The waiting crowd dreads the sound of the calling of their name because they know they will have to walk up to the throne and face their final destiny. The good news is that God's children have no reason to be in that waiting throng. Neither do they have anything to dread. Those who have a relationship with God will just close their eyes for an instant in death and open them in the sunlight of God's heaven. The relationship will not change, only the surroundings.

Some have the image that the judgment is going to be like a huge set of scales with all their sins on one side and all their good works on the other. They breathlessly await the verdict to see which side outweighs the other because it determines their eternal destiny. This is a works-based standard of judgment which is contrary to what God explains to us in the New Testament. Paul tells us clearly, "It is by grace you have been saved, through faith. . . it is the gift of God, not by works so that no one can boast" (Ephesians 2:8). It is vitally important for every Christian to realize that God credits the righteousness of Christ to us so that it's not our own good works but His that gives us eternal life (Romans 4:24). When God looks at sin-stained lives, He doesn't see our sinfulness. Through His blood-colored lenses He sees us pure as snow because our sins have been wiped away and our feeble works, however inadequate, have been replaced by the righteousness of Christ.

In Matthew 25, in the judgment illustration given by Christ, all people are separated as a shepherd divides the sheep from the goats. In Palestine, the sheep were white and the Syrian goats were dark, so Jesus was making the point that a decision was not necessary. It was obvious to the shepherd which animals went into the sheep pen and which were herded into the goat pen. It was an easy task which could be done even in the dark. The judge immediately said to the sheep which were on his right hand, "Come you who are blessed by my father; take your inheritance, the kingdom prepared for you since the creation of the world." There was no examination of the sheep's words, deeds, and thoughts. The judge did not search through the "book of life" to see if their names were written therein because he knew them by name and ushered them lovingly into their eternal reward.

In the great, white, throne judgment scene painted in Revelation 20, something similar happened. "Death and Hades gave up the dead that were in them and each person was judged according to what he had done. Then death and Hades were thrown into the lake of fire. The lake of fire is the second death." If death and Hades were all cast into the lake of fire, where were the righteous souls who had died? The author believes that those who were in the "book of life" never stood before the great, white throne. They had a special exemption from God's judgment. Revelation 20 was written in figurative language to describe Satan's doom and the destruction of all his followers. Those who had a relationship with God were already enjoying the continuation of their relationship in heaven while the judgment of Satan and his people was taking place.

The Greek word for judgment (*krima*) is the same root word as condemnation (*katakrima*) which means "judgment against." Paul said emphatically in Romans, "There is now no condemnation for those who are in Christ Jesus, because through Christ Jesus the law of the Spirit of life set me free from the law of sin and death" (Romans 8:1). In this passage, Paul says there is absolutely no condemnation or judgment against those in Christ in this world or in the next. If there is no condemnation for those in Christ, is there any reason for them to appear before God in judgment?

A Glorious Restoration

God's ultimate purpose throughout the Bible is to restore to His children the relationship He had with man in the Garden of Eden described in Genesis 2. In the middle of the garden was the "tree of life" which gave its inhabitants the power to live forever. After man's sinful fall, we do not hear about the tree of life again until the last chapter in Revelation where God paints a figurative picture of heaven as a beautiful city where His children will "reign for ever and ever" (Revelation 22:1-5). The Bible, in its entirety, allows us to see God's macro-plan which allowed man to fall from grace, but provided a savior to restore mankind to eternal happiness. The reason God sent the prophets and eventually His own Son to die for man's sins was to call man back to a relationship with Him. God is a god of reconciliation and restoration not separation and estrangement.

In the Garden of Eden, God enjoyed walking and talking with Adam and Eve in the cool of the evening. That's where my book started. Those who have a relationship with God can enjoy this precious experience in this life as well as the life beyond. On this earth we talk with God through prayer and He talks with us through His Spirit and His revealed Word. In eternity, He will talk with us face to face as father and child.

In the Garden of Eden, there was no sickness, no sorrow, and no death. Adam and Eve and their descendants could have lived forever had it not been for sin. In Revelation 22 we read of a restored paradise where there is no night, no sickness (the leaves of the tree of life will heal the nations), and no curse of death. Imagine a city that needs no electricity or sunlight because God is its everlasting light.

God has accomplished many amazing restorations throughout history. He restored the Israelites back to the Promised Land. He restored sinful, lost people to a state of reconciliation through the cross of Jesus. He has restored His church from apostasy and extinction time and time again. But the greatest restoration of all will be when God restores those who have a personal relationship with Him to their long-awaited eternal home.

The New Testament closes with the words. "Blessed are those who wash their robes that they may have the right to the tree of life and may go through the gates into the city. . . The Spirit and the Bride say, 'Come!' And let him who hears say, 'Come!' Whoever is thirsty, let him come; and whoever wishes, let him take the free gift of the water of life" (Revelation 22:14-17).

A personal relationship with God is indeed a free gift that every person in the world is invited to receive. God invites us to travel with Him as we journey home. The author hopes this book will be instrumental in causing many to desire an eternal relationship with God.

1. What role does death play for the person who has a relationship with God?

2. Is God's final judgment an evidentiary trial or a sentencing hearing? Explain your answer.

3. Describe your view of the great "white throne" judgment?

4. What does it mean that God looks at us with "blood-colored lenses"?

5. Why are sheep and goats a good illustration to describe the Judgment?

6. Since both come from the same Greek word, what is the difference in judgment and condemnation?

7. What is God's purpose throughout the Bible for those who have a relationship with Him?

KNOWING GOD IS ETERNAL LIFE

I heard about a woman who checked a book out of the library only to find it dull and uninteresting. Later, as the story goes, she fell in love with the author and became his wife. She started the book again and discovered to her surprise that she liked it. She thought it was one of the best books she had ever read. What changed her attitude toward the book? She had a relationship with the author. What a difference a relationship makes in our perspective.

There is a big difference in "being religious" and knowing the author.

In John 17:1-3 Jesus looked toward heaven and prayed: "Father, the time has come. Glorify your Son, that your Son may glorify you. For you granted Him authority over all people that he might give eternal life to all those you have given him. Now this is eternal life: that they may know you, the only true God and Jesus Christ, whom you have sent."

Jesus prayed earnestly for his apostles to know God. Knowing God meant a lot more to Jesus than knowing about God. Knowing about God is intellectual. Knowing God is relational. Knowing God means to be personally and intimately acquainted with God. The King James Version of the Bible used the word "know" to describe the intimate relationship between a husband and wife. "Adam knew Eve and she conceived." The apostles knew who God was before Jesus called them, but they lacked a real relationship with God.

As you come to the close of this book you have learned a lot about the God who seeks relationship. You have learned about the spirit's fire, the power of prayer, God's nourishment, and the benefits of a relationship with Him. My sincere prayer, as the author, is that you have not only learned about God but have come to know God personally and intimately as Jesus intended.

Jesus said, knowing God is eternal life. The eternal life of which He speaks, is not something that comes after we die. Jesus used present tense not future tense. It is here and now. It begins when we first develop a relationship with God and lasts throughout our lifetime and eternity. You can taste eternal life today, on this earth, by truly knowing God and having a relationship with Him. Our eternal life simply continues in a new house as we transition from earthly life to spirit.

The apostle Paul made a statement similar to Jesus' prayer in Philippians 3:10. He said, "I want to know Christ and the power of

His resurrection and the fellowship of sharing in His sufferings, becoming like Him in his death." Isn't it remarkable that this veteran apostle with over 30 years preaching experience still wants to know Christ? Again, knowing Christ is not just knowing about Christ but having a personal relationship with Christ—becoming more Christlike. Since Christ and the Father are one, a relationship with one is a relationship with both. To know Christ in this way is to take up your cross and follow Him even if it leads to suffering and death. Paul's journey involved both suffering and martyrdom. Paul made the superlative claim in verse 8 that, "I consider everything a loss compared to the surpassing greatness of knowing Christ."

Once the apostles had a true relationship with God their lives changed. No one can be in the presence of Christ and remain the same. These ordinary fishermen and a tax collector walked with Jesus for 3 years and turned the Roman Empire upside down. I'm sure they begged for a few more years of training but Jesus, the Master Teacher, believed they were ready. There is no limit to what ordinary Christians can do when they are totally devoted to God.

Intellectuals don't like the word "relationship" because it sounds too emotional and "feeling." They prefer the expression "knowing God" but Jesus clearly used the term "knowing God" to mean relationship. I believe the word relationship is more relevant today because we talk about knowing computer science when we mean knowing about computer science. You can't have a relationship with computer science. You can only have a relationship with an intelligent, loving being.

Knowing Christ, as Paul says, is the essence of Christianity. We should all desire to have a relationship with Christ and become like

Him. It's not enough to have a relationship with a church as we saw in chapter 6. We must have a relationship with Christ Himself. It's possible to have "churchianity" instead of Christianity. Churches help us grow and have a lot of essential ministries but it's possible to spend so much time in meetings and committees debating doctrines and activities, that we miss the precious relationship that Christ wants us to experience.

Liberty Instead of Legalism

I was fascinated as I stood in Philadelphia's Independence Hall and observed the cracked Liberty Bell, a symbol of America's freedom. The bell tolled for the first public reading of the Declaration of Independence in 1776. It cracked beyond repair at George Washington's birthday in 1846. The bell bears the biblical inscription, "Proclaim liberty throughout all the land unto all the inhabitants thereof "(Leviticus 25:10). This Scripture refers to the Year of Jubilee which occurred every fifty years in Israel.

Christians don't have to wait fifty years to experience freedom. Paul declared that "Christ has set us free." Jesus said, "The truth shall set you free." How can Christians hear these words and not be stirred by the powerful message of liberty and freedom? I never heard these messages in the church of my youth. I sincerely thought I had to keep every rule in the Bible perfectly or I would be lost. I practiced a works-salvation religion that made God into a tyrant instead of a loving father. When one reads the Scripture from the perspective of God's grace the whole Bible takes on new meaning. I have learned that one's entire Christian life is a thanksgiving offering to God. God accepts us and saves us because we are his sons and daughters even with all our weaknesses and failures. We don't have to be perfect to go to heaven. Hallelujah! What a sense of freedom that brings.

As God accepts us, His imperfect children, He also wants us to accept our brothers and sisters in spite of their weaknesses and opinions. He wants us to be dispensers of liberty and grace to others. Jesus told a parable about the unforgiving servant who, after receiving grace himself, took his fellow servant by the throat and choked him before throwing him into prison (Matt. 18:21-35). Do you think Jesus could have foreseen anyone in His kingdom acting this way? Paul taught grace toward our brothers and sisters in Romans 14 when he concluded that a Christian could be a meat eater or vegetarian, an observer or non-observer of religious holy days, a wine drinker or abstainer and it didn't matter to God so one should not condemn his brother over matters of personal liberty. Those who have a true relationship with God are liberty-loving people.

Over the past year we have seen freedom-loving people in Egypt, Libya, Syria and other Middle Eastern countries demonstrate for liberty and even give their lives for democratic change. I see a parallel in organized religion as Christians raised in legalistic churches are reading The Grace Awakening by Charles Swindoll, searching the Scriptures for themselves, and learning for the first time what they never heard in the church of their youth. God promises us liberty from man-made laws, traditions, and creeds. God gives us the liberty to draw our own conclusions and to disagree with the guardians of our faith. We also have the liberty to decide how to best use our time, talents and money to serve others and advance the cause of Christ.

There is always a danger people will misunderstand what true liberty is. Liberty is not promiscuity--it is not a license to sin. A person who has a personal relationship with God will not want to sin. Sin dishonors God and hurts us as well. Paul explains the paradox of how Christians can be free and be slaves at the same time. "Now that you have been set free from sin and have become slaves to God, the benefit you reap leads to holiness and eternal life" (Romans 6:17-18).

Liberty does not mean freedom from responsibility. When a 16 year-old driver takes the car keys he needs to realize the awesome responsibility that goes with driving. We have the liberty to glorify God with our lives at all times. We have the liberty to be pure because God lives in us. We have the liberty to love others as we would like for them to love us. This is the golden rule.

Truth Instead Of Tradition

Jesus' timeless challenge echoes down to us today. "You shall know the truth and the truth shall set you free" (John 8:32). This verse is the motto of the Christian university where I taught for decades. This is one of the boldest claims Jesus made. No human being knows all the truth on any subject and sometimes we have genuine disagreements over what the truth is. It's alright to disagree. Peter and Paul disagreed. We must learn to disagree in love. The pursuit of religious truth can be very dangerous. Speaking the truth cost Jesus his life...as well as James, Peter and Paul. Truth did not set them free in a physical sense, it only hastened their death. When one speaks the truth, sooner or later he is going to have a collision with a time-honored tradition and consequences will follow. Dedicated ministers have been fired and churches have been split because they dared to make waves against tradition. When truth and tradition clash brotherly grace is usually in short supply.

Jesus spoke clearly on the subject of tradition. "The Pharisees and teachers of the law asked Jesus, 'Why don't Your disciples live according to the tradition of the elders instead of eating their food with unclean hands?' He replied, 'Isaiah was right when he prophesied about you hypocrites; as it is written: These people honor me with their lips but their heart is far from me. They worship me in vain; their teachings are but rules taught by men. You have let go of the commands of God and are holding on to the traditions of men.' And he said to them, 'You have a fine way of setting aside the commands of God in order to observe your own traditions'" (Mark 7:5-9). Jesus went on to give an example of how they created a tradition which allowed them to circumvent one of the 10 Commandments.

Will the truth set you free from persecution, suffering, hardship, and pain? No. The truth will set you free from ignorance, prejudice, legalism, fear, and sin. Every Christian must search for the truth in God's Word and in his own heart even it leads down roads which are less traveled. A conscientious Christian should stand up for the truth even if it runs against the comfortable grain of church tradition. But those who have a relationship with God will speak with grace and love. There are good traditions and bad traditions. Oh, that God would give us the wisdom to see the difference. We must resist becoming a slave to tradition like Tevye in "Fiddler on the Roof." "We've always done it that way" is a poor reason to support any practice. It's important for every Christian to know the difference between tradition and divine truth.

The Pharisees were zealous about their traditions but Jesus said their worship was vain. They would even kill in the name of tradition. They observed all the traditions religiously but rejected Christ because he did not fit their mold. He was a threat to their traditions. They drew a circle around themselves and all those who were faithful to their traditions and Jesus did not fit inside that circle. We should constantly be on guard lest we become modern-day Pharisees. The key to eternal life is not found in following tradition but in knowing God and pursuing a relationship with Him.

I hope every reader will find a closer relationship with God—not in being more religious, but in truly knowing God and His Son. Time spent with God is never squandered. God is inviting you to share eternal life with Him. You should want to know Him personally and intimately. You can have a relationship that never ends. God is inviting you to join the adventure.

1. What did Jesus mean by "knowing God?"
2. When does eternal life begin?
3. How important was it to Paul to "know Christ?"
4. How can Christians be free and slaves at the same time?
5. List some things from which the truth shall set you free? Can you think of more the author did not give?
6. Why does a works-salvation make God into a tyrant?
7. Define the term "grace dispenser." What steps do you need to take to become a better "grace-dispenser"?
8. What happens when you take liberty too far?
9. What is bad about tradition in religion? What traditions might be good and healthy?
10. Why can the truth be dangerous?

www.ingramcontent.com/pod-product-compliance
Lightning Source LLC
La Vergne TN
LVHW051126080426
835510LV00018B/2259